Resorts of Maldives

THIRD EDITION

Written and photographed by Adrian Neville

SevenHolidays

1	2	3	4	5	6	7	8	9	10		1	2	3	4	5	6	7	8	9	10

LOWEST RELATIVE PRICE HIGHEST   MOST   ROOM DENSITY   LEAST

T Telephone F Facsimile
E Email
Website

Foreword

Every picture was taken on the resort that it illustrates, apart from the underwater shots. I have used these with the resorts that are particularly renowned for their diving. None of the photographs have been altered in any way. What you see is what you get.

I look forward to building the most comprehensive, the most independent and the most engaging website for holidays in the Maldives. I hope to meet you there in the future on sevenholidays.com.

KEY

Flying

Speedboat

Dhoni

A beer

1.5ltr water

Lime juice

Full day island hopping

Sunset fishing

Dive centre

Single dive

5 x Multiple dives

PADI Certified Open Water course

Notes on the Information Box

I have added the service charge (usually 10%) onto prices wherever I know it is implemented. However, I haven't got complete knowledge on who does and doesn't charge it. Indeed, some resorts don't add a service charge at the time of purchase but add a blanket 10% charge on the final bill.

As to dive prices, I have tried to state the price of a dive and multiple dives with all equipment and the boat trip(s) included. Where I have relied on information from the resort or dive base, I can't guarentee that this has always been done. Similarly, not every dive base has added in the 'certificate price' in the cost of their Open Water Course. The price quoted is meant to be for all lessons, equipment, boat trips and the certificate.

For the **room density** scale I have divided the exact size of the island by the number of rooms on it (and off it, where there are waterbungalows). Some resorts have a number of rooms that are not on the official list but are used at least for over-booking situations. This would mean that they are, in fact, more 'dense' than indicated. Other islands are, in effect, more 'dense' because guests are restricted from sometimes large areas of the island.

Different nationalities get different prices and different packages for holidays on the same resort. My **relative price** scale is not going to be accurate for everyone but it is a good general indication of how much a holiday will cost there in relation to the other Maldives resorts. I have given an average 'price' where an island has more than one resort. Those resorts are Kurumathi (3), Kuredu (2), Meedhupparu (2) and Meeru(2).

Contents

Introduction

Location

The Republic of Maldives lies in the Indian Ocean an hour's flight southwest of Sri Lanka and India. From the northernmost island to the southernmost it stretches 860 kilometres down the 73°E line of longitude to just below the equator.

Geography

The archipelago consists of 26 atolls sustaining 1,192 islands. Of these, 198 are inhabited. A sizeable majority of the islands are under 500 square metres in area. The fourth largest is less than three square kilometres and the largest (Gan on Laamu Atoll) is just over five square kilometres.

Three quarters of the islands are less than one and a half metres above mean sea level. 80% are less than one metre above mean high tide.

Population

The total population of the country is just under 300,000, of which nearly half live on Male, the capital. It is envisioned that the new island emerging from the lagoon of the airport island, Hulhule, will become a second Male - hence its name Hulhumale - and put an end to the capital's overpopulation.

Every Maldivian is a Sunni Muslim and speaks Dhivehi, although the southern atolls have a distinct dialect.

Climate

The year round temperature is consistently between 26°C - 30°C. Two distinct seasons divide the year. The Northeast Monsoon (essentially a wind direction) runs from December through to April. This is the tourist high season when there is little rainfall, open blue skies and constant sunshine. The Southwest Monsoon runs from May through to November. During this period it is still generally dry and sunny but with sporadic rain and cloud cover. It is only at the turn of the two seasons that the weather can be persistently inclement. That is November into December and May.

At least that is how it has always been. You will not be surprised to read that the weather has become far less predictable in the last few years.

Local time

GMT + 5 hours

Clothing

Light cotton clothes are ideal. Any length of shorts, tops and swimwear is acceptable on the resort islands, but nudity is not allowed. A couple of sets of smarter wear for the evenings is a good idea but never de rigueur (except on one or two Italian resorts).

When taking a local island visit or a trip to Male it is recommended that longer, less informal, clothes are worn, out of respect for Maldivian sensitivities.

Money and credit cards

For a thousand years and more the predominant medium of exchange in the region was the cowrie shell (Cyprea moneta) which was farmed exclusively in the Maldives.

Today the Maldivian Rufiyaa is the national currency. Its value is tied to the US Dollar, with an exchange rate of $1 = MRf 12.85. There is no black market. Tourists tend to do all their business in US Dollars, though most resorts will happily accept Euros.

Maldives is now set up to accept all the major credit cards. Every resort expects you to pay by credit card (the top resorts have mobile GSM terminals that go to the guests), and all the shops you might visit in Male and even many of the shops on 'fishermen's islands' are happy to accept them.

There is an ATM in the airport arrival hall (on the left just before the exit door) and more than ten on Male. There is very little need to come with cash, a credit card will almost always be sufficient.

Communications

The international country code is +960.

Mobile phones work on every resort island. Upon arrival your handset will display the name of the network that has been automatically selected. One of the network companies is called Wataniya and the other is the established landline provider, Dhiraagu. You can manually select your preference.

Dhiraagu offers a few more services, such as accessing your voicemail and dialing from your phonebook without the need for additional codes, and the ability to make local calls at premium local rates rather than international rates. It also has a good English language customer care service available 24/7 by dialing 123.

3

PERFUMES & SKINCARE
where else would you go?

BVLGARI (cacharel) Calvin Klein CHANEL Christian Dior CLINIQUE *Davidoff*

DKNY dunhill EMPORIO ARMANI ESCADA ESTÉE LAUDER

GIVENCHY GUCCI BOSS ISSEY MIYAKE Jean Paul GAULTIER KENZO

LACOSTE LANCÔME Laura Biagiotti L'ORÉAL MONT BLANC paco rabanne

RALPH LAUREN ROCHAS TOMMY HILFIGER

LeCute
Majeedhee Magu, Malé

LeCute
Duty Free - Malé International Airport

quality most compare

Arrival

Just as every resort island is a single hotel, so Hulhule island is nothing but the airport. It sits a short distance off the coast of Male like a huge aircraft carrier. You fly in and take a boat or a seaplane out to your resort.

A full flight and a busy morning will mean several minutes queuing. The formalities themselves are straightforward. There are no specific requirements for entry and everyone gets a free 30 day visitors' visa. It is worth noting here that malaria has been successfully eradicated from the country.

The following items are prohibited: alcohol, drugs, pornography and idols of worship. People caught with illegal drugs are particularly harshly dealt with. Other items will be confiscated and returned to the guest when he or she leaves.

If you land without a booked holiday you can go to the Tourism Ministry's Information counter inside the airport building, you can enquire from the many individual resort booths that line the exit, and you can negotiate with representatives from local travel agents. But almost certainly the price you end up paying will be more, often much more, than the price available from a tour operator in Europe.

Outside the terminal you will be met by your tour operator representative who will tick you off a list and sort out the transfer to your resort. Otherwise you make your way to your resort's booth for the same service.

There are three modes of transfer: the dhoni (local boat), the speedboat and the seaplane. The seaplane is the king of transfers because it is a wonderful experience in itself. The flight on a cloudless day is as memorable as it is unique. Speedboats are fine for the short to middle distances, except on the few rough days in the year (when the bigger the better). Dhonis are not much used for transfers now but the slow rhythm of this fine traditional craft soon helps to ease out the fast pace of life the tourist has brought with them. It's Maldives pace from now on.

Departure

Daytime flights from the airport are straightforward but nighttime flights often mean leaving your resort many hours before departure. The reason is that the seaplanes are grounded after 6pm and only nearby resorts are happy to do boat transfers, owing to the danger of hidden reefs.

A half-day Male excursion is the ideal way to use up the time profitably. Sensibly, these are often scheduled to coincide with night flights, but I reckon a half-day at any point in the holiday is time worth spending to check out the sights, shops and citizens of this unusual capital, throbbing with nearly half the country's total population.

If you have time on your hands but not enough for a Male trip the airport hotel has a swimming pool and plenty of outdoor tables for snacks and drinks. The Captain's Bar inside is the friendly 'local' and good food is served at the two restaurants. The hotel runs a convenient shuttle bus to and from the terminal.

Inside the terminal building there isn't much to do except wait and shop, but the bonus is that the shopping is surprisingly good. If you came away from your resort without a souvenir or pulled back from that jewelry purchase, you get a last chance here. But more interesting are the shops that you don't find on the resorts, offering prices well below those on the high streets of Europe.

For famous brands in watches, electronics, fashion and beauty products it might be worth your while holding back a little of that holiday budget. You can't take back a piece of Maldives - it's illegal - but you can go home with a bargain Tag Heuer, Suunto dive computer, Givenchy handbag or the new Isse Miyake perfume.

By my count there are presently 92 resorts with 11 more due to open in 2007. The 92 takes into account the three on Kuramathi, Veligandu Huraa's two, the 'picnic island' Dhoni Mighili and Equator Village on Gan in the deep south.

What's the difference?

It's amazing just how different one resort can be from another. To be honest, it's also amazing how just about everyone who comes to the Maldives has a great holiday no matter where they end up. But if you put some thought into what you would like to have on your island and what you would rather not find there, and then find it in this book, you are on your way to a truly memorable couple of weeks. Here is a list of the main things to consider as you surf for your ideal 'getaway':

Some islands have a policy of getting a mix of nationalities but most resorts tend to have more of one nationality than any other. And a few resorts are all Italian. Even if you love the sound of a particular island, it may be a mistake to take your holiday there.

Although there is a dive base on every single resort and although there is no such thing as a bad place for diving in the country, some islands are much more focused on diving than others. If you are a keen diver these are the ones to seek out. There will be more frequent diving on offer, more options available (such as night diving, double tank and all-day safaris) and more fellow divers to share your experiences with.

If you don't dive but you're a keen snorkeler then you want to find a resort that has a surrounding reef with at least some of it close to shore. It is at the drop-off that you'll find the greatest variety and density of fish. If you are a beginner or a nervous swimmer then any fair-sized lagoon will do for you. A really close reef drop-off wouldn't be ideal.

For learning watersports a large, deep lagoon is best. For watersports experts, look for the few resorts that have large set-ups and active staff (I have tried to indicate in the book which these are).

For the sun worshipper, well, you can't miss. But do you like to have a lot of people around for the fun, games and evening activities or are you looking for a private spot and early bed? The Maldives is great for both, but read up to make sure you don't make a terrible mistake.

A number of islands take just a few minutes to walk right around, others are relatively huge. Some don't have much in the way of vegetation and coconut palms (but wonderful beaches); others have towering green interiors and picturesque palm trees leaning out over the water (but maybe unsightly groynes and sea walls).

The Maldives is one of the truly great holiday destinations of the world. The variety it offers under the sun and under the water will keep you coming back for years, checking out one resort after another looking to find that perfect paradise. If it is to be found anywhere on this earth, it might well be here, somewhere...

They say there are two Maldives, Male and the rest of the country. Any comparisons between the simple, quiet life of the islands and the competitive vigour of this pocket-sized capital are becoming more and more tenuous every year. Male has just under half the country's population. It is the funnel through which almost all political, social and economic activity passes, trickling out to the 'fishermen's islands'. It is as rich, as modern and as forward thinking as anywhere in South Asia. A half-day visit will give you the flavour of the place and a chance to check out the historical highlights and do a bit of shopping.

Along the waterfront you will find the not-to-be-missed fish market with its tiled floor covered by regimented, glassy-eyed tuna and the occasional hammerhead shark or swordfish. Next door to this is the exotic fruit and vegetable market and some 'car boot sale' stalls. Further along is Republic Square, the 'public face' of Male, with its flagpole, pigeons and park benches. Walking away from the square, you pass the imposing President's Office, a couple of ministries and a line of prestigious office buildings. With the ferries and transfer boats constantly maneuvering in and out, this is the political and economic centre of the capital.

'Trends', the outdoor café/restaurant of Nasandhura Palace Hotel, is a natural place to end the walk, but if you carried on around the corner of the island you would find the recreational centre of the capital. An artificial beach and swimming pool is surrounded by open spaces for official celebrations, team games and play areas for mothers and children, who pack the place out after sundown.

A 'block' behind the waterfront are situated most of the important historical sites: the modern central mosque, the old Friday Mosque with its fantastic coral carvings, the first presidential palace next to the mausoleum of the saint who converted the country to Islam, and the museum in Sultan's Park which used to be a small part of the palace grounds. An informative guide is a great help in appreciating these places, but beware of those whose main aim is to steer you as quickly as possible to the shops where they get a commission.

Most of the tourist souvenir shops are conveniently located on a single road, Chandani Magu, that leads due south from Republic Square where the majority of visitors disembark. As many of the shops sell the same or similar items, it is worth checking out a number of them to be sure that the price you are offered is competitive.

Strolling around, you will likely come across famous brands in fashion, consumer electronics and beauty products, but a word of caution: as in any other Asian city, there are plenty of fakes, copies and rip-offs around. The big four shops that deal in genuine articles only are Reefside, Evince, Le Cute and Sonee Sports. Reefside is prominently located at the top end of Chandani Magu and Evince is down towards the end of the road. Evince and Le Cute (which is just around the corner from Chandani Magu, on Majeedi Magu) are very impressive set-ups. It will come as a pleasant surprise, even a shock, to most visitors that Male has such state-of-the-art shops with such classy products.

Male has gone from being the capital of an isolated sultanate, closed in on itself, to being a vibrant city open to the world, as modern-minded and as market-oriented as any great city in the region. If you get the chance to spend half a day here, don't miss it.

Business hours
The government sector works from 07.30 - 14.30 without a break (except for tea time around 11.00) and then closes down for the day. Private businesses more or less stick to a 09.00 - 17.00 day, while shops open between 09.00 and 10.00 and don't close until they are legally required to do so at 23.00. Tea shops can stay open until 01.00.

The Dives

Almost every dive in the Maldives is a drift dive. This is a wonderful, effortless way of watching the underwater world pass by. With the current coming into the atoll bringing fresh, clear water the visibility might be fifty metres and the big pelagics might be queuing up to watch you pass by. But, on the other hand, there is an ever-present danger, however small, that a current will take you away from the atoll and out into the deep blue. It is the job of the instructor (often with the help of an experienced dhoni captain) to assess the local conditions before any diver jumps in the water. It is a tribute to the professionalism of the dive centres that accidents have been extremely rare.

The Coral

Few divers paid much attention to the corals when they went diving in the Maldives, fish was what they were looking for, particularly the big ones: whale sharks, sharks, mantas, turtles, napoleon wrasse, tunas...Then, in 1998 widespread coral bleaching occurred due to a too warm sea that moved around the Indian Ocean. Suddenly people noticed the crumbling, grey stone walls where once, they remembered, there used to be colour. The fish numbers never decreased but some of the beauty of a dive had gone with the corals. Now the corals are back. And divers are not just looking at the fish but also checking out the coral regrowth. A field of young, pink soft coral swaying in the current is a new delight, as is the sight of pristine white juvenile hard corals and new coral breaking out of the cracks of an ancient brain coral. Brand new species to the Maldives are being discovered and identified.

The Fish

There is a greater density of fish and a greater variety of fish in the Maldives than just about anywhere else in the world. Furthermore, there are laws and regulations in place that protect those fish and their environment. Most other dive regions have laws and regulations too but in the Maldives they are adhered to and that is not so common. The Maldives is also fortunate in not having to cope with the livelihood demands of a large and fast-increasing population. What we have here is a true diving paradise. Please do your bit to keep it that way.

Dive Centres

Every resort has its own dive centre. Almost across the board the equipment is new or nearly new, the brands are top-of-the-line and the maintenance is first class. You can be confident of hiring everything you need. If you prefer to bring your own wetsuit a half-size 3mm one is enough, unless you are going to do more than one dive a day. The water is consistently between 27°C and 30°C. Every dive centre offers open water certification and some form of introductory or discovery dive.

The area where one dive centre differs from another is in service. I don't just mean loading and unloading the baskets from the boats and talking to the guests in the evening, but also things like information and presentation of the local habitats, the number of divers per boat/instructor, the variety of dive sites on offer each day, the type of diving on offer (multi-dives, full-day, night diving, nitrox, etc.) and the amount of effort put into learning and adjusting to new guests' standards and preferences. The dive company's website is one place to start to find out what's on offer, and then it's a matter of word of mouth, reputation, and this book.

Anantara

Anantara (South Male Atoll)

Anantara, a company with several fine resorts in Thailand and expanding in the region, has taken over and is now running the three resorts that are grouped here together. Dhigufinolhu is now called Anantara, Veligandu Huraa is now called Naladhu and Bodu Huraa remains so named. The long walkways that connected the resorts has been dismantled and little boats ferry guests around. They are free to move between the resorts to sample the different restaurants and bars and make use of the facilities. I imagine that access to Naladhu would be somewhat restricted.

Bodu Huraa is their four star property, which is sold exclusively to the Italian tour operator Hotel Plan. It is made up of 36 Over Water Villas and 14 Deluxe Over Water Villas (with in-room espresso machine). It is an active place with daily and nightly activities and entertainments. Facilities include championship tennis, squash and badminton courts; volleyball is a given. Relaxation is around the 25 metre infinity pool and in the Reflections Spa.

Anantara

Anantara Resort is their five star property. Of the 110 room total, 70 are Deluxe Beach Front Villas (two with a pool) and 40 are Over Water Suites (two with a pool). The four restaurants on the island offer a choice of Italian-led Mediterranean fare, Thai-led Asian fare, Maldivian and International cuisine. The facilities include a large infinity pool, spa, fitness centre, championship tennis court, watersports (non-motorised is free) and dive centres.

Anantara

Naladhu is their six star resort. There are just 19 villas set on a beautiful garden island with an impressive stand of mature coconut palms in the middle. Each villa has its own little infinity pool, the latest and finest in design and amenities and a designated butler on call day and night. All the facilities and restaurants of the other resorts are open to these guests, while on this island is an exclusive restaurant/lounge, a gym and a yoga pavilion.

The group of three resorts is just 35 minutes by speedboat from the airport, set in a very large and beautiful lagoon. The lagoon has created wonderful beaches on the resorts but at low tide it can be very shallow. Pools have been created just off shore. For snorkeling, guests need to take a trip out, as the reef drop-off is too far to reach and is open to the ocean. However, this is one of the prime diving areas in the Maldives. Just a few minutes away are a wreck, a manta point, a shark point and spectacular caves.

T: 664 4100 F: 664 4101
E: infomaldives@anantara.com
www.anantara.com

Biyadhoo (South Male Atoll)

The beautiful island of Biyadhoo has been taken over by the company that runs the very up-market Coco Palm resorts and Makunudu. At some point in the future, then, it is likely to rise steeply in quality and price but at present it remains an excellent choice for an economical diving and snorkeling holiday.

Biyadhoo

The island has one of the best resort housereefs. It is close to shore almost all the way around, with lots of coral growth inside the lagoon as well as down the drop-off. There's also good topographical variety to the reef. The diving in the region is famous for sites such as Kandooma Thila with dense schools of fish, Kandooma Caves with soft corals and the Protected Marine Area of Guraidhu Kandu (a broad channel).

Biyadhoo with Villavaru behind

The beach comes and goes around the island but there is plenty for everyone and good opportunities to find your own hideaway beach between the palms and bushes. There are few other resorts with coconut palms taller or more dense than they are here.

The decline of the resort in the last few years of the previous owners has been turned around with good maintenance and the upgrading and re-styling of interiors. The infrastructure remains essentially the same, with accommodation in six two-storey blocks of eight rooms above and eight below. The corner rooms are slightly larger and will take three or four beds for a family. The blocks are all beach fronting with decent shade cover.

There is just the one restaurant serving buffets and set menus to the guests who all come on full-board basis. The main bar is close by and faces the sunset, while a second, more distant bar has been set up as an evening music venue.

T: 664 7171 F: 664 7272
E: sales@sunland.com.mv
www.biyadoo.com

Coco Palm Bodu Hithi (North Male Atoll)

Boduhithi and Kudahithi were formerly all-Italian, Club Vacanze resorts. They are now a part of the prestigious Coco Palm Collection. After major reconstruction, Coco Palm Bodu Hithi is now finding its place among the country's five star resorts.

On this medium sized island, with its good natural growth of tall palms, are just 44 Island Villas. Generously sized, they are well equipped inside with flat screen tv, sound system, designer fixtures and attractive bathroom. A private courtyard hides a pool, day bed, sundeck and shower.

On the water are three categories of villas: 16 Water Villas, 16 Escape Water Villas and 24 Escape Water Suites. All are equally well appointed and vary mainly in size. The largest rooms, the Escape Water Suites are set furthest away from the island and have their own restaurant and bar - The Stars. A round-the-clock butler service is also for their exclusive use.

Wining and Dining is accented on this resort. Apart from The Stars there are five other bars and restaurants, from the all glass venue 'Wine Bar' to the seafood 'Aqua' over water and the al fresco 'Breeze', where guest can enjoy casual à la carte dining and, a fun innovation, cooking for themselves. Special dinners for two are also set up on sand banks and desert islands, or while cruising.

The Coco Spa offers treatments from Indonesia, Thailand and India and utilise a collection of ayurvedic inspired skin care products. There are also yoga and tai chi pavilions as well as the fitness centre. For more strenuous exercise there is a tennis court and a badminton court.

For those who need to bring a little work with them, Bodu Hithi also has a high-speed internet connection and a modular space for meetings for 6 - 20 people at a time. Secretarial facilities are included too.

T: 664 1122 F: 664 1133
E: boduhithi@cocopalm.com.mv
www.cococollection.com.mv

Coco Palm Dhuni Kolhu (Baa Atoll)

Dhuni Kolhu, the original Coco Palm resort, has garnered a series of awards for its environmental achievements, its water bungalows and its overall quality. Set amidst tall palms on an island encircled by a perfect beach, an ideal lagoon and a fine reef drop-off, it is no surprise that it is gaining a strong reputation and firm loyalty from its repeating guests.

Shaped like an elongated 'D', the reef is close by all along the curved side, whilst the straight side faces west to a deeper lagoon that is ideal for watersports, and those romantic sunset cocktails, be it the Conch Bar on the beach or the swim up Lagoon Bar on stilts over the water.

This is an island for relaxation and also for activity. Apart from the watersports, there is a recreation centre that offers tennis, table tennis, badminton and a gym, as well as indoor games and audio visual room, a bar and jacuzzi. The excursion list is also long and varied. If one day you have an intimate champagne breakfast for two on a desert island beach, another day you might choose to join a Maldivian family in their home and help prepare a traditional dinner after strolling together around their island. You might even join a Maldivian tuna fishing boat for a day's pole and line fishing.

The 98 rooms are mostly made up of Beach Villas (58) and Deluxe Villas (26). Both categories are the same size and vary in luxury details - a four-poster bed, a splash pool and sunken bath in the garden - and positioning on the slightly quieter east side close to the snorkeling.

The 12 Lagoon Villas are also the same size but are more luxurious still in terms of the furniture and materials used. Half of them look north and half of them look south. At the end of the jetty, facing sunset, proudly sit the two Lagoon Palace Suites. These are almost twice as big as the other rooms and boast outstanding, uninterrupted views, perfect privacy and a high level of luxuries. Guests can upgrade to these rooms just for a night at a time, when they are available.

T: 660 0011 F: 660 0022
E: dhunikolhu@cocopalm.com.mv
www.cocopalm.com

Coco Palm Kuda Hithi (North Male Atoll)

This is one of the truly exceptional island in the country. It is very small and very exclusive. Indeed, you couldn't get more exclusive. There is only one villa on the whole island. Every aspect of the "resort" is designed to appeal to seriously wealthy clients searching for ultimate experiences.

The Island Residence has, of course, its own butler. That is not so uncommon in the top echelon of resorts. But no other resort in the country has a 3 star Michelin chef to personally cook for you - whatever you want and whenever you want it.

A word to the butler and any event or activity is immediately organised, be that cruising, desert island picnicking or overnighting, deep sea fishing or diving. However, the island is so peaceful and the residence so large and luxurious that most guests will spend a large part of their holiday in their own realm.

If you wish to have a spa treatment, your therapist will come to your residence and use the special spa area. The residence is very large indeed, including the sea view deck and integrated pool. It is also designed to be completely hidden from the world outside. All the roofs are thatched and the interior is the latest in contemporary design.

T: 664 0143   F: 664 8877
E: kudahithi@cocopalm.com.mv
www.cococollection.com.mv

Coco Palm Dhuni Kolhu   Coco Palm Dhuni Kolhu

Coco Palm Dhuni Kolhu

Coco Palm Dhuni Kolhu

Four Seasons, Landaa Giraavaru

Four Seasons Explorer

Four Seasons, Kuda Huraa

Four Seasons at Kuda Huraa (North Male Atoll)
Closed for a full two years after the tsunami of December 2004, the original Four Seasons in Maldives is back with a resort that promises the best of elegant living combined with a relaxed, village feel.

The 25 Beach Pavilions, 32 Beach Bungalows and single Royal Beach Villa each have walled tropical gardens surrounding their open-air shower, courtyard and pool. Bougainvillea, Bird of Paradise flowers and Frangipani blossoms across the island give the whole resort a garden feel.

The 32 Water Bungalows, four Navaranna Water Bungalows and two Two-bedroom Water Bungalows have untrammeled views to the sea from the bedroom and bathroom. While the deck can only be seen from the sea so is perfect for sunbathing.

All the rooms are designed to compliment their surroundings with a modern tropical style of openness and impeccable simplicity.

The resort rightly prides itself on its marine research projects and community projects. Guests are invited to join a variety of cultural events both on the resort and the neighbouring fishing village. They are just a few of an exceptionally wide range of activities and excursions. A quite unique offering is the surf school, running courses for beginners, surf clinics and escorted surf excursions for the experienced.

Perfectly in line with the homely, village feel, the resort is very family friendly. Several of the rooms have interconnecting gates and verandas and there is an extensive Kuda Mas Kids' Club. On top of that you have a staff that is as effortlessly helpful as is possible to imagine. I found the legendary Four Seasons service to be just that.

It must be said that the beach is mostly man-made and not of the finest quality. The lagoon is very large and shallow, which is fine for swimming but guests take the free boat trips to enjoy some snorkeling.

The huge infinity pool is a great asset with its clear views and its swim-up bar. Nearby is the Café Huraa serving contemporary Asian, Western and barbecue food al fresco. Here too is the dinner only Baraabaru Restaurant serving fine Indian cuisine. Away from the buzz, the Reef Club serves up Italian fine dining. All this is complemented by a wine cellar of finest handpicked vintages.

Finally but far from least, the Island Spa occupies its own private island a minute or two away by dhoni.

T: 664 4888 F: 664 4800
E: reservations.maldives@fourseasons.com
www.fourseasons.com/maldives

Four Seasons at Landaa Giraavaru (Baa Atoll)

This second Four Seasons resort in Maldives opened at the end of 2006 and is another landmark in the progress of the country's tourism. Set in a beautiful corner of undeveloped Baa atoll, the resort combines its legendary service standards with a rare level of sensitivity to its human and environmental locality.

In the traditional Maldivian manner (but using recycled material), each villa domain is entered through a turquoise gate in a whitewashed coral wall. Swimming pools are the courtyard around which open, thatched rooms nestle. Hi-tech paraphernalia does not find a place here. Deep relaxation and inspiring beauty is what this is about.

The green interior has been left alone as much as possible, to compliment and contrast with the vast, empty lagoon and the neighbouring deep channel. A number of environmental initiatives are carried out by the Marine Research Centre and a marine biologist gives talks and accompanies snorkelers.

I am not sure of the quality and accessibility of the snorkeling at this stage but the lagoon is ideal for swimming and watersports. There is an array of motorised sports and all non-motorised sports are free of charge. Diving in the region is still completely uncrowded and, to some extent, still in its infancy.

The country's very first land and ocean villas are the prime rooms. The two double-bedroomed Koimala Land and Ocean Villas, which can be combined as a single estate, have beach and over-water accommodation connected by wooden walkways. For the rest there are three categories of land villas (bungalows on the north side, villas on the south side) and three categories of water villas (either sunrise or sunset).

The Landaa Spa has a special Ayurvedic Retreat set up by experts from Kerala, and a resident yogi to guide beginners and the advanced.

Rather unusually there is a kid's club and a young adults club, indicating the child-friendly attitude of the resort. What is absolutely assured for everyone is a caring, personalised service of the highest standard.

T: 664 4888 F: 664 4900
www.fourseasons.com/maldives

Fun Island (South Male Atoll)

Fun Island closed down after being affected by the tsunami. The resort (which is one of the Villa group of hotels) will be completely broken down and rebuilt but, as yet, there are no definite plans to what that it will look like. It could become another five star resort or it could fill a space in the three and four star market.

Located in the middle of a huge lagoon (neighbouring Olhuveli), there is no nearby snorkeling but it is ideal for swimming and watersports. At the top end of the lagoon is the Guraidhoo Channel, which is a world class dive site.

Giravaru (North Male Atoll)

The resort closes in March 2007 for a year or so. It will be completely broken down and built up again as a very smart, contemporary but 'classic' sort of resort. An up-market brand of hotels will oversee the transformation and take on the management of the new property. It will have approximately 80 rooms and won't be in the top bracket in terms of pricing but perhaps not far below.

The proximity to the airport is in its favour but it has a headache in dealing with the sight of the growing 'rubbish island' between Male and itself. This should be successfully dealt with by building most of the rooms as water bungalows behind the island and looking out to sea. The island itself is nicely positioned at the edge of its own circular reef, with a fine lagoon, good snorkeling and easy access to many, well-established, dive spots.

T: 664 0440 F: 664 4818
E: giravaru@dhivehinet.net.mv
www.giravaru.com

Halaveli (North Ari Atoll)

Halaveli had a long history as a lovable Italian resort. To some extent it was a relic of the early Maldives tourism with its coral walls and thatched roofs, its modest looks and its special atmosphere. The new Halaveli is due to reopen in December 2007 and it will be very much in the mode of the modern, five star, chic Maldives tourism.

With sister hotels at the very top end of the market in Mauritius, the remade Halaveli promises to look stunning and provide a level of service to vie with the best already in Maldives. The rooms - all still thatched but now with wooden and terrazzo flooring - will be divided into Beach Villas with one Presidential Beach Villa and Water Villas with six Stand Alone Water Villas that can be linked to make up a Presidential Water Villa. The total of 83 rooms on this small to medium sized island does, however, give it a density figure at the cusp of two and three on my scale.

The island itself is D shaped and a beautiful beach runs all the way around it, extending at the two points into huge tongues of pure, white sand. The lagoon has a deep side and a shallow side that suits the waterbungalows, watersports and swimming. The reef comes close by for a couple of hundred metres and although it doesn't offer the best snorkeling to be had on resorts it is easily accessible from the beach.

Diving will always be a key ingredient to this island. A couple of economical full-on dive islands are in the neighbourhood and Halaveli will be the luxurious way to enjoy some of the country's best dive spots. A short boat ride away are four Protected Marine Areas - two major shark points and two spectacular thilas. A good number of channel dives are also just a few minutes away.

The resort's spa looks likely to be another big draw, offering 12 double treatment rooms and a long menu of pleasurable and regenerative treatments.

Guests will be arriving on bed and breakfast basis and then avail themselves of the three very different restaurants. The main restaurant will serve international buffets for all three meals, the specialist restaurant on stilts over water will offer an à la carte fusion of East meets West and the beach grill will be a smaller place for daily fresh surf and turf.

The new Halaveli will probably turn out to be more beautiful and just as lovable as the original.

T: 666 0559 F: 666 0564
E: mkt@constancehotels.com
www.constancehotels.com

Halaveli

Halaveli

Halaveli

Hudhu Ran Fushi (North Male Atoll)

Opened in early 2007 after extensive remodeling, this island formerly called Lohifushi, is now a good-looking, four star resort promising top value for money with an abundance of activities and smart, contemporary rooms. As well as the expected sports facilities, the resort has tennis, squash, badminton and a gym.

A relatively large island, it easily accommodates the 137 beach bungalows with unobstructed views to the beach. And being a mature island of lush vegetation, privacy between the rooms is assured. Historically, however, it is not an island with a great beach everywhere. The west side, facing into the atoll has decent beaches held by frequent groynes while the east side, facing the ocean, has some beach and a good deal of coral stones. Judicious sand-pumping may change all this. It is on the southeast side that the surfers congregate for some excellent, predictable breaks.

There is lots of lovely, soft sand in the lagoon, which is great for swimming and watersports. It is too large for housereef snorkeling but the management puts on (charged) snorkeling trips. In the lagoon are 30 waterbungalows that are almost half as large again as the beach bungalows and are, as usual, the prime rooms. Well-appointed, wooden and thatched, these are fine rooms that fit in with the Maldivian landscape, as indeed do the beach bungalows.

Diving has long been a big part of the resort and this should continue, although numbers do tend to drop off when a resort becomes all-inclusive. The dive sites are all well-established but still good, with a great variety of destinations within an hour's dhoni ride: from channels, thilas and outside dives (think whale sharks) to caves and wrecks.

Finally, at just a half an hour's speedboat ride from the airport this born again resort island should do very well.

T: 664 9130 F: 664 9131
E: info@hudhuranfushi.com.mv
www.hudhuranfushimaldives.com

Hudhu Ran Fushi

Kudarah

Hudhu Ran Fushi

Kudarah

Kandooma (South Male Atoll)

Closed after the tsunami of December 2004, the resort has been taken over by the people who have Cocoa and Rihiveli. There are no projections available for when it might reopen, or when, indeed, work will begin on what will surely be a complete remodeling.

Kudarah (South Ari Atoll)

Since completing the photography and review, this resort has been sold on by the Italian company Club Vacanze to Yacht Tours, the company that sold their island, Dhonveli Beach, to John Keells of Sri Lanka (who already run Hakura Club and Velidhu). Whatever the machinations of the trade these days, the fact is, it won't be an easy task to transform this island.

Where once there was a beach all the way around, today there is just one small area of beach at one end of the tiny oblong island. The rest is a rocky shoreline. It is remarkable that the island had such a lovely beach because it is located in the mouth of a large, fast channel and it only has a very small lagoon for protection. It must be possible then that the beach can be restored and retained.

Ideally the resort will be a haven for people looking for a small, quiet resort that is sophisticated and is well-serviced but doesn't offer all the trappings of modern technology and the high life. We will have to see what emerges after renovation.

The housereef is just a few metres away and top-rated diving is all around in this southeast corner of the atoll.

Machchafushi (South Ari Atoll)

Diving remains key to this small island near to the famed channels of southeast Ari Atoll. Reopened in late 2006, the German dive company Subaqua is back to run the diving efficiently but also with imagination and flexibility. Apart from the great pelagics in the channels, there are the schools of fish and varied corals around the many thilas just inside the atoll. Prime among these is the Protected Marine Area Kudahrah Thila.

Escorted and unescorted dives around the housereef are possible at any time of day. And, despite the many months of resort reconstruction, the housereef is still one of the best in the region for diving and snorkeling.

The number of rooms has jumped up from 58 to 86 with 16 Superior Beach Front rooms, 42 Deluxe Beach Front rooms, 18 Over Water Suites and 10 Paradise Villas (over water). The resort as a whole is described as 'unpretentious cosmopolitan'. It is well-placed in the middle bracket of pricing, offering good quality and choice at a reasonable price. German speakers would be the largest single group in a broad mix of European guests.

The new Machchafushi runs as a sort of up-market all-inclusive place. There is almost no restriction on beverages (sparkling wine and cocktails are included) and the changing snacks available all day and night amount to varied meals in themselves.

So back it comes, Machchafushi, expanded and modernised, offering that successful mix of a mid-priced, easy-going all-inclusive with first class snorkeling and diving.

T: 668 6868 F: 668 6869
E: machchafushi@dhivehinet.net.mv
www.machchafushi.com

Mahureva

Mahureva

Mahureva

Mahureva (North Male Atoll)

This is the original Valtur island in the country. It's sister island is Kihaad on Baa Atoll, which is the more expensive version of this fun club concept. Everyone comes on an all-inclusive package and the food is predictably Italian and excellent.

Mahureva is on the island of Gasfinolhu just 30 minutes up the east of the atoll from the airport by speedboat. There isn't much to the interior of the thin island but it's clean-swept look and lily-lined paths between the bungalows are pretty.

All the activity during the day happens on the main beach and the lounge bar that are located on either side of the jetty. As all the watersports are free and the day and night are filled with organised activities, everybody congregates in this area and quite clearly has a great time.

The beaches on the other, ocean, side of the island are quite small but fine nonetheless and perfect for getting away for some quiet time. The reef drop-off is too far away for snorkeling and diving is not a particularly popular activity here. The large lagoon is just perfect for things like aqua aerobics, swimming around and generally just enjoying your fellow guests in the pristine, turquoise waters.

T: 664 2078   F: 664 5941
E: respgest@mahureva.valtur.it

Makunudu (North Male Atoll)

Makunudu has the charm of a traditional Maldives look and feel. Where once it was at the top end of the market, it has been passed by quite a number of ultra modern, chic resorts with their state-of-art interiors and gadgets. Makunudu prefers the genuine warmth of service and an appearance in tune with the region.

The rooms are each decorated with a small Thundu Kunaa grass mat, which is the finest craft produced in the Maldives. White walls and drapes set-off the mixed brown tones of timber, cane and whicker. A woven mat ceiling keeps up the thatched roof. The bathroom is outside, in the Maldivian 'giffili' style.

The 36 rooms on this lovely, small island are tucked into the rich vegetation but always just a few feet from the shore. The beach is wide and wonderful for a good part around the island but not everywhere. The snorkeling is good and easily accessible. With relatively so few guests, the dive staff get to understand and work with divers as individuals, responding to their level, wishes and requests.

The style of service is always remarked upon here. "Couldn't be more friendly and helpful" is a common comment. Guests are made to feel at home.

In the spirit of being at home, breakfast is served at your room, out on your verandah or beach. For some nationalities holidays here are all-inclusive but that's not the case for all nationalities so issues can occasionally crop up. Overall, Makunudu continues to deliver a delightful, very Maldivian holiday.

T: 664 6464 F: 664 6565
E: makunudu@sunland.net.mv
www.makunudu.com

Makunudu

Makunudu

Makunudu

Makunudu

Makunudu

Medhufushi

Medhufushi

This resort also closed after the tsunami at the end of 2004 but has stayed closed due to legal wrangling between the owners. It is likely to reappear sometime in 2007.

Villivaru (South Male Atoll)

This resort, on the next door island to Biyadoo, has closed down and changed hands but the new owners have no plans, or no plans as yet revealed, to redevelop the island.

W Maldives

W Maldives (North Ari Atoll)

The new resort on Fesdu island represents a fresh departure point for the Maldives. W Hotels have a very high profile across North America and the Maldives now hosts what is described as their premier resort. A distinct look, a different style of service and new ideas have arrived alongside some brand new guests.

W's philosophy of "Whatever/Whenever" suits the Maldives perfectly. Although children are happily accommodated it's essentially an adult atmosphere where "Acceleration and Deceleration" can happen at your will. Acceleration means getting stuck into, for example, diving, big game fishing, kite surfing and the state-of-the-art gym. Deceleration means meditation, yoga and the spa, offering ayurveda, shiatsu and aromatherapy as well as the massages and beauty treatments.

I'm not sure which word describes time in the nightclub, '15 Below'. The three bars and three restaurants are perhaps the most distinctive in look and feel. As for cuisine, 'Kitchen' is a modern take on Bistro dining, 'Fire' offers casual but grand barbecue feasting (spit-roasted lamb and suckling pig) and 'Fish' is the signature restaurant serving up the best in fish and seafood cuisine, over water of course.

The more traditional Maldivian look of the rooms from outside is contrasted with ultra chic, contemporary interiors. This means custom made furniture and all modern gadgetry, such as surround sound and a 42" plasma tv. The outdoor living area has day beds, a plunge pool, shower and personal barbecue.

A majority of the 78 rooms are over water, which is sensible for an island that is beautiful and small. It is fortunate to have good soil for tall palms and flowers. The beach is fine and wide all around the island and the reef is not only easy to reach but was one of the best for snorkeling.

The resort has a marine biology station that organises guest education programs, presentations and guided trips, which is all good news. Guests will be delighted with the quality and variety of the dive sites in the neighbourhood. A fine wreck dive is a few minutes away, one of the best island reefs is a few more minutes away and, within 40 minutes, four Protected Marine Areas can be reached.

T: 332 9489 F: 334 1646
E: reservations.wmaldives@whotels.com
www.starwoodhotels.com

W Maldives

W Maldives

W Maldives

In order to keep up with the number of tourists wishing to come to Maldives, 46 islands will become new resorts between now and 2011. And in order that every part of the country gets the chance to benefit from tourism, these resorts will be spread throughout the country. Every atoll will have at least one resort.

11 islands have already been given out and are just opening or are about to open. The islands are Alidhoo on Haa Alifu; Hodaafushi on Haa Dhaalu; Dholhiyadhoo on Shaviyani; Maavelavaru and Randheli on Noonu; Kalhufahalafushi on Thaa; Olhuveli on Laamu; Funamudua and Hadahaa on Gaaf Alifu; Konotta and Lonudhuhutta on Gaaf Dhaalu.

Of the other 35 resorts 20 have been bid for while 15 are reserved for a proposed public company for tourism development. The idea behind that is to allow ordinary Maldivians, who can't hope to bid for an island, to buy shares in a company that will have resorts.

The 20 resorts have been split into two batches of ten resorts in order to stagger their development. Furthermore, ten of those 20 are for 'lease-rent controlled bids' and ten are for 'lease rent open bids'. Previously, all bidding was open and those companies that bid highest usually won the bid. This led to an imbalance of more and more expensive resorts. The 'lease-rent controlled bids' are there to ensure that there will be a sufficient number of medium sized resorts for the medium priced charter markets.

These are the names of the islands and their atolls for the first batch of ten. First the five lease-rent controlled islands: Manafaru on Haa Alifu; Kudamuraidhoo on Haa Dhaalu; Kudafunafaru on Noonu; Malefushi on Thaa; Vatavarreha on Gaaf Dhaalu. And then the five lease rent open islands: Vagaru on Shaviyani; Lundhufushi on Raa; Meradhoo on Gaaf Alifu; Munandhuva on Gaaf Alifu and Gazeera on Gaaf Dhaalu.

These are the names of the islands and their atolls for the second batch of ten. First the five lease-rent controlled islands: Kabaalifaru on Shaviyani; Gaakoshibi on Shaviyani; Medhafushi on Noonu; Kanifushi on Lhaviyani; Elaa on Thaa. And then the five lease rent open islands: Naridhoo on Haa Alifu; Maanenfushi on Raa; Gasveli, Dhekunuboduveli, Kudafushi (three in one) on Meemu; Mahadhoo on Gaaf Alifu; Kaishidhoo on Gaaf Dhaalu.

A Shangri-La resort hotel is planned for the large island of Viligili on Addu Atoll. It has gone through various stages of dispute and construction and doesn't have a firm opening date at this time.

Finally, something completely new. The first hotels to be built on inhabited islands are planned for Fuamulak (which is its own atoll just above the bottom atoll, Addu), Hankede on the Addu Atoll causeway and possibly one other on Addu Atoll. At this stage they are not certain to go ahead but, if they do, they would represent an entirely new aspect to tourism in Maldives.

| 1 | 2 | 3 | **4** | 5 | 6 | 7 | 8 | 9 | 10 |

LOWEST   RELATIVE PRICE   HIGHEST

| 1 | 2 | **3** | 4 | 5 | 6 | 7 | 8 | 9 | 10 |

MOST   ROOM DENSITY   LEAST

T 666 0587   F 666 0558
E bir-front@bathala.com.mv
www.bathala.com

North Ari Atoll

 20 mins

$3.85

$3.85

$3.30

1/2 $18

$15

Bathala

$57

6 x $332

PADI $522

ADAARAN Club Bathala

This resort has a mix of two-thirds club Italians and one-third quiet life Germans.

Each is doing their own thing separately on this very small island, resulting in a distinct lack of togetherness and atmosphere. It's just not one thing or the other.

It used to be a place where Germans came to holiday simply and cheaply and go diving as much as possible. The diving in the area is excellent but the long time base leader left in 2005 as the number of divers went down in relation to the increase in Italian guests.

The Italian guests are all with Azemar and enjoy their own animators, evening cabarets and film nights. They certainly have a good time but can't quite let loose and do their own thing.

One thing that everyone likes, of course, is the beach and Bathala is fortunate in having a very good one around almost the whole island. And with almost all the rooms having great views out to the beach and the lagoon, this is an ideal place for lounging on your verandah in the shade and then taking a few steps out for sunbathing.

A few more steps through the lagoon and guests can enjoy some of the best housereef snorkeling to be had on a resort. Being on the edge of the atoll, the reef is visited by or is home to a host of schooling fish, turtles, tunas, eagle rays, napoleon wrasses and even, I am told, hammerhead sharks.

For those who dive, the rewards are big. The two nearby highlights are the Protected Marine Areas of Maaya Thila, which has been described as "the white tip reef shark capital of the Maldives", and Fish Head, described as "the grey reef shark capital of the Maldives". The latter has also been adjudged one of the ten best dive sites in the world!

Although this could no longer be described as a dive island, the quiet atmosphere, early nights and lack of requests for excursions and entertainments still persist. On the other hand, the Italian guests are organised by their own animators for excursions, fishing and evening entertainments in a separate building (formerly the reception).

In a similar sort of way, the restaurant has plenty of space for tables for two, which the Germans prefer, but the Italians enjoy long tables and large groups at dinnertime. One evening buffet is the 'Italian night', while at each of the other, decent but not inspiring, buffets there is a 'pasta corner'.

The 46 rooms are, like the resort as a whole, simple and straightforward. They are clean, comfortable and air-conditioned but don't include any extras, such as a hairdryer or even a telephone. Calls can be made at the reception. Most of the rooms have excellent locations on the beach but several are tucked behind and don't have views.

In truth, it appears that reinvestment and maintenance have not been a priority over the last number of years and there's no sense of enthusiasm about the island coming from the management. It is not the cheap gem of a place it used to be but the beach and the snorkeling are still very rewarding.

1	2	3	4	5	6	7	8	9	10
LOWEST		RELATIVE PRICE			HIGHEST				

1	2	3	4	5	6	7	8	9	10
MOST			ROOM DENSITY					LEAST	

T 664 2688 F 664 2035
E front@rannalhi.com.mv
www.clubrannalhi.com

South Male Atoll

 45 mins

 150 mins

 $4.40

 $4.40

 $4.95

 $60

 $20

 Venta

 $72

6 x $393

PADI $545

ADAARAN Club Rannalhi

I Viaggi del Ventaglio fill most of the rooms on this resort. Their other resorts worldwide are called Club Venta, hence Club Rannalhi, and the club concept is central to the resort's daily life.

However, there is a varying ratio of other nationalities, particularly French and German, at different times and so the mix and atmosphere change.

Apart from the French, German and British, Chinese, Singaporeans, Japanese and others occasionally take rooms, as the resort runs a nighttime airport transfer for the late Asian flight arrivals. To some extent this is a cosmopolitan resort that can offer a private beach holiday but the dominant ethos is the Italian club scene.

There is some sort of activity and music throughout the day and into the night. It could be aqua gym, boca, volleyball, Latin dancing, quizzes or a number of other fun, participatory events. The active watersports centre on the communal beach offers canoeing, windsurfing, water-skiing and banana boat rides.

The diving school is large and surprisingly busy. The instructors are enthusiastic and clearly the guests are enjoying their diving. Snorkeling is also popular here. The reef is accessible around two-thirds of the island, the coral is growing back strongly and the fish highlights include white tip reef sharks, eagle rays, jacks, turtles and passing dolphins.

The beaches are also good for about two-thirds of the island but the south side of the island, which is the main 'get-together' beach, has had to have a series of groynes built to counter erosion. And on the western end, behind the waterbungalows, a wooden walkway has been built where the sand has disappeared. The lagoon retains its lovely sandy bottom, so the swimming is perfect - and the snorkeling is never far away.

An issue for some people will be the number of rooms. The reception, restaurant and coffee shop are gathered together in a spacious area, with fine sand in between. But the 100 land rooms are in tightly packed, two-storey blocks. Then there are 16 waterbungalows as well, with more planned. If you are gregarious (read Italian club) you might think this is just fine, otherwise you might not.

The blocks are made of concrete, but they are attractively painted. Inside, they are of a reasonable size, pleasantly decorated and with good fixtures and fittings, including a hairdryer and a large multichannel tv. The waterbungalows face west to the sunset but, sadly, they have one of the smallest sundecks anywhere - and the privacy is not great.

The restaurant is large, with a rather grand, almost formal, look, which lends an air of importance to mealtimes. And the quality of the food does not disappoint. The buffet spreads are extensive and very nicely prepared. The waiters are attentive, the chefs genial and the general chatter encouraging. There is, of course, an Italian chef to overlook the live pasta preparation.

One bonus for the Italians is a resident biologist who conducts walks around the island talking about the natural environment (including a fine banyan tree). This is a welcome feature which should happen more often elsewhere.

| 1 | 2 | 3 | 4 | **5** | 6 | 7 | 8 | 9 | 10 | | 1 | 2 | 3 | **4** | 5 | 6 | 7 | 8 | 9 | 10 |

LOWEST   RELATIVE PRICE   HIGHEST   MOST   ROOM DENSITY   LEAST

T 658 7700 F 658 5500
E admin@meedhupparu.com.mv
www.meedhupparu.com

Raa Atoll

 45 mins

 240 mins

$4

$3

$2

$25

$15

Divepoint

$57

6 x $300

PADI $500

ADAARAN Meedhupparu

Developing its own identity and adapting to changing market conditions, Meedhupparu remains a big success.

The underlying reason for this is simply value for money. You can enjoy the dream of Maldives here at a very fair price.

There are also significantly different ways to enjoy it. The Italian market, through Franco Rosso, used to dominate but, since 2005, that is no longer the case. Italian animators do continue to shepherd their guests with welcomes at the entrance to the restaurant, with a series of daily activities and a separate cabaret and disco. But increasingly the club concept is hard to maintain here and will probably be phased out. That is not to say that the Italian market will disappear, merely change.

The majority of guests are now British and Germans enjoying the Maldives the way they like to. That is to say without animators but with plenty of fun and new found friends in the bar, around the pool and down the beach. Having said that, the place is generally for quiet and relaxation. There are evening entertainments in the bar (Boduberu, crab race and karaoke) but they never take over. Indeed that would be impossible as the bar is so large, with such a high roof, that it doesn't seem to fill up or really generate a great atmosphere.

The same is true of the large restaurant and reception but it doesn't seem to matter much as the food and the service are good. For a change from the three buffets a day there is a reasonably priced fine dining restaurant nearby.

Alongside these two groups of holidaymakers are two more, quite distinct: one in the waterbungalow village and the other in the ayurvedic village.

The waterbungalow village is brand new. It has its own jetty, reception and restaurant and is planned as a separate five-star entity for a different sort of holiday on the same island. We will have to see how that develops.

The ayurvedic village is certainly something different and, so far, unique to the country. The Sri Lankan company that runs the resort has brought over qualified and experienced personnel to ensure that it is not merely a trendy concept.

The rooms are built in a rustic style and set apart from the rest of the rooms. A consultation with an ayurvedic doctor will give you advice on which package of treatments and massages would be most suitable for you. And then those treatments can be had either within the village or in the ayurvedic area of the public buildings, which is open to everyone. Swiss guests seem to particularly go for this bit of Meedhupparu, but every guest should at least avail themselves of a consultation and some advice.

The beach is great most of the way around the island, with just some erosion problems in the southwest corner. At the water's edge, the beach slopes down fairly sharply to give an immediate swimming depth but little width for paddling around. The lagoon bottom is smooth and sandy and the reef drop-off is always within swimming distance. The snorkeling is good but not great.

The same might also be said of the diving. For some reason there doesn't seem to be quite as much to see as in other atolls. As this is the only resort in the atoll, however, the sites are untouched and there is no chance of meeting other dive boats, which is good compensation.

The land rooms are all the same and fine but nothing special, although they do have a tea and coffee maker, hairdryer and safe. Built in C-shaped blocks and surrounded by vegetation not many of them have views to the sea but neither are they far away.

All in all, this is a large, simple resort that doesn't promise too much but delivers a good package of price and facilities in one of the world's most beautiful spots.

Vaavu Atoll

 35 mins

 120 mins

 $3

 $3.50

$3.50

1/2 $17

$17

Alimatha

$52

5 x $260

PADI $533

Alimatha

Few resorts in Maldives feel as good as Alimatha. All Italian (through Alpi Tours), it's a club set-up that everyone has bought into.

The management is relaxed, the animators bronzed and friendly, and the children happily supervised.

The resort is not just for families, far from it, but it does cater for children unusually well. Of first importance is the attitude of the staff to children and here it's faultless. Then it's a matter of facilities and activities. There isn't a swimming pool but the lagoon is nice and shallow and also large enough to be untroubled by waves and currents.

The children's mini-club has both morning and afternoon sessions, while the adults are on the beach sunning or, often, getting together for aqua aerobics, fun and games. Uniquely there's also a children's theatre time immediately after dinner and before the adults' entertainment, when they can take part in organised singing and dancing and dressing up. It's quite clear that the kids are having a great time. In the restaurant they aid and abet the convivial flow between the tables.

The buffets are impressive and the restaurant well positioned near the water's edge. Its high roof is thatched and the floor either wood or sand. There is a carafe of wine on the table and the self-service draught beer and soft drinks are complimentary. Everyone is on the same full-board arrangement.

The main beach is very large and in the right place - facing south and near the jetty, reception and watersports centre, from where the music is pumped out. The west side has some beach but the rest of the island has a low wall between the sand and the water for protection against further erosion.

Some of the tallest palm trees of any resort are on Alimatha. The island looks lovely from the sea. The bushes between the rooms and the beach, however, have been cleared so it is light above and the views to the lagoon are unimpeded.

Without much vegetation around the rooms, the privacy is reduced but that is not much of an issue on this island. Many guests prefer to leave their sliding glass doors open and bring their wicker chairs out onto the verandah the better to enjoy the natural and human sights and sounds.

Inside the rooms are comfortably large enough to take another bed or cot. The furniture is not fancy but it is all you need. The mirror is large, the shower pressure is good and the overall maintenance is very decent.

In 2006, 34 Waterbungalows were opened to add to the 96 Beach Bungalows. The new total of 130 rooms pushes to the limit the beach space (and restaurant capacity). It could be a problem if the clients here weren't as gregarious as they so obviously are.

There are surprisingly few inhabited islands on this atoll and they are not nearby, so there is just one half-day trip a week to visit one. On the other hand, there is a full day and even an overnight trip to a desert island. Sunset fishing happens every day and snorkeling trips happen twice a day, which is very good.

There is good snorkeling to be had on the resort too but it is not an extensive area. Around the jetty the corals are growing back well and you can find lobsters, barracudas, stingrays and black tip reef sharks, amongst much else.

The dive base enjoys a prime position next to the watersports centre on the main beach and this would help explain why it is so busy. A surprising number of Italians here go diving regularly. Another reason would be the dive base leader, who has been here for nearly ten years and is still enthusiastic, friendly and attentive. With only one other resort on the atoll (and few inhabited islands) the dive sites are fresh and rewarding.

Alimatha is a fine resort. It happily describes itself as three-star and delivers a five-star atmosphere.

1	2	**3**	4	5	6	7	8	9	10

LOWEST   RELATIVE PRICE   HIGHEST

1	2	**3**	4	5	6	7	8	9	10

MOST   ROOM DENSITY   LEAST

T 668 0510   F 668 0520
E *angaga@dhivehinet.net.mv*

South Ari Atoll

 30 mins

 $3.30

 $3.65

 $3.85

 $37

 $17

 Sub Aqua

 $58

6 x $312

PADI $514

Angaga

For the natural things Maldives has to offer, Angaga is lucky indeed. Palms, beach, lagoon, snorkeling and diving are all first class here.

Add to this a quiet, laid back atmosphere and you can see why it's a big hit with the Swiss and German clientele. The one downside is that the interior design and build is not nearly up to the standards of its natural setting.

In a time when more and more resort beaches are getting help from groynes and walls, Angaga's beach still goes all around unobstructed, pure and fine. There is some evidence that the added waterbungalows might change things but it's not happening yet. With a soft, sandy lagoon on one side and good shade on the other, this is really a beach to savour.

Life on Angaga is slow-paced and very quiet. There are few evening entertainments and daytime excursions, but most people seem content to break up their day with beach walks, snorkeling, meals and verandah lounging.

The first dive sets off at nine o'clock, which is most unusual for a Swiss and German island. And the full-day trip is from nine to four, not eight to six, so people can get back to the beach and verandahs. That is not to say the dive school is slack. On the contrary, this is a busy, friendly and extremely well run base. It is not for nothing that it has won The Best Divebase in Maldives award from Tauchen magazine.

"Every year we have to do a little bit more", says the base manager Jochen. Having signed up the night before, divers just walk onto the boat come dive time and, with a maximum of 16-18 per boat, there's plenty of space. Each diver gets a bottle of water and a towel. There's a fresh water showerhead and, on one of the two boats, a sundeck and toilet. In the high season in particular there's a high percentage of repeaters, adding to the amicable, family atmosphere.

As to the diving, Angaga is within striking distance of all the sites on the east, west and south of South Ari Atoll. To the west is a famous Manta Point, to the east are the channels and thilas and outside the southern islands are the places to sight whale sharks.

Oddly the dive base is the only place with a painted tin roof, completely out of keeping with the other buildings, which are all attractively thatched. Having said that, the good looks are sadly not repeated inside the public buildings or the rooms. The reception is inappropriately 'grandiose', with vaulted ceiling and a big tiled, raised platform in the middle. On the other hand, the coffee shop, bar and sunset bar look patched up and down-at-heel.

The 50 Beach Bungalows make much use of bamboo and plywood and the main lighting is from fluorescent tubes. The shower is large, though, and the water pressure high. The best part is the cool, dim verandah outside, with its Maldivian swing bed.

The 20 Water Villas also lack style and quality but they do at least have a lovely sandy-bottomed lagoon for swimming. Those facing northwards don't catch too much sun on their verandah but the reef is accessible. The others face south for the daytime sun.

The reef drop-off runs close by for two thirds of the island - just check the direction of the current for a drift snorkel from the jetty. One direction will take you all the way around to the steps of the sunset bar, at the end of the water villas. The coral life is OK but the fish life is excellent. "There are loads of turtles, we've stopped photographing them", said one happy snorkeler, "we got buzzed by four white tip reef sharks last night, at the change of shift".

Another highlight is the dining, especially at night, with candlelit tables and sand underfoot below the arched, thatched roof. The plates are big and so is the buffet selection. Chefs line up to serve and cook at the live stations. The spread is fantastic, but one tip here: it doesn't change that much so better do only some of it each night.

If you're not put off by style issues or you don't intend to spend much time indoors anyway, Angaga is really a lovely island - very pretty, very quiet, with a great beach and fine snorkeling.

1	2	3	4	5	6	**7**	8	9	10
LOWEST		RELATIVE PRICE		HIGHEST

1	2	**3**	4	5	6	7	8	9	10
MOST		ROOM DENSITY		LEAST

T 664 3502 F 664 5933
E maldives@angsana.com
www.angsana.com

Images down left side courtesy of Angsana

North Male Atoll

30 mins

$6.50

$3.50 (1ltr)

$7

1/2 $35

$25

Marine

$98

5 x $490

PADI $691

Angsana Ihuru

When the Banyan Tree company took over its neighbouring resort of Ihuru the standard of the human environment went up dramatically but the already almost perfect natural environment was sensibly left alone.

Angsana might be seen as the youthful sibling of Banyan Tree. Their high standards and their philosophies are similar but for subtle reasons they are attractive to different people. Angsana looks younger and more modern, almost funky, with its zestful colour scheme of citrus yellow, earthy orange and the green of a fresh bamboo shoot.

A lighter touch to the service and in the atmosphere is noticeable, in part the result of a clientele that is younger and less accustomed to having only the finest things in life. In part it is the result of a happy group of staff who are mostly Maldivian, have worked on the island for many years and who love it as their own.

The essence of Angsana is simple luxury and a fine spa on an idyllic island. Appropriately, the spa is very big relative to the size of the island. Its eight luxurious double pavilions cover an extensive area behind the rooms. They are usually busy as the guests take seriously the island's motto of 'sensing the moment' and succumb, frequently, to the sensual pleasures of a great massage. Therapeutic touch and aromatherapy treatments are the spa's specialities.

The rooms represent simple luxury. Although a little small for such a quality resort, they are very attractively put together and have the added touches of a hairdryer and bath robes, coffee and tea-making facilities and a CD player. Of the 45 total, 20 villas come with open-air jacuzzis behind. In front, each room has a swing joli in a small garden made private by enclosing bushes and trees. And from inside every room, through the wall of French windows, you can see the beach and lagoon. Unlike a growing number of resorts, there is no staggering of rooms on Angsana.

The resort is popular with peace, quiet and privacy seekers. Daytime sees some use of the complimentary watersports facilities and an uptake on excursions (admirably there is a guide for every couple going to Male) but there are no organised entertainments in the evening, not even television, it's not that sort of place. Nonetheless, the bar is a delight as the navy blue sky deepens into night, and the lights of Male flicker on the horizon. Spotlights around the perimeter, hanging lamps above the bar and candles on the low tables help create a truly cosy, privileged feeling.

The bar's lovely deck over the water is matched by the even broader restaurant deck. It's an idyllic place for lunch (always buffet) and dinner (six fine set plates and one Maldivian buffet), though the quality of the cuisine is not quite matched by the wine list.

The perfect geography of the island itself has already claimed many awards and the commendably green attitude of the owners (the resort has won two in ten of the President's Environment Preservation Awards) should ensure more to come. After a global search the beach was named the second best beach in the world in a recent book on the subject. And if that wasn't enough, the housereef has been named by Asian Diver, and is generally agreed to be, the best resort housereef in Maldives.

Over 140 fish species and an abundance of living coral at the steep drop-off and inside the lagoon that is neither too big nor too small, make this a snorkeler's dream. For a sun and beach dreamer it is equally good: an unbroken, broad, fine, white sand beach. There are no groynes or walls at all, only temporary sandbagging on alternate sides of the island to counter the free movement of the sand over the two seasons. Pumping, however, has been used to shore up the depleted side and, over time, this less fine sand has brought the beach quality down from perfection. Nonetheless, this is now one of the best small resorts in the whole region.

T 676 0028   F 676 0029
E reservations@velavaru.com
www.velavaru.com

Images above and right courtesy of Angsana

Dhaalu Atoll

35 mins

$6.50

$3.50 (1ltr)

$7

½ $35

$25

Marine

$98

5 x $490

PADI $691

Angsana Velavaru

Some islands have a sense of calm and tranquility that you feel almost the moment you step off the landing jetty. Velavaru is one of these.

There's something in the air that makes the place a bit special. It doesn't try to do too much: either to continually entertain or to provide numerous options. It keeps it all very simple, as simple as the essential Maldives.

At the end of 2006 the resort was relaunched as a second Angsana in the country. This is the younger, more chic sibling to the Banyan Tree brand. The essential changes to the original resort are the refurbishment of the villas, the restaurants and the spa, plus the inclusion of a marine centre. The improvements are in just the right areas and we now have an even finer resort.

With trademark touches of lime green and tangerine, the villas now have a fresh, contemporary look and feel. The rounded shape opens up the space and is a welcome contrast to the common rectangular design. The total number has been reduced to 79 and consists of 28 Beachfront Villas, 30 Superior Beachfront Villas with Jet Pool, 18 Deluxe Beachfront Pool Villas, two Velavaru Villas and one Angsana Villa. The more expensive rooms mostly, but not always, have the best combination of privacy and beach. In some parts of the island the intervening vegetation can be a bit on the thin side.

The thatched, dome-shaped roofs and natural materials used on all the buildings integrate the resort nicely into the landscape, making for an ideal setting. There is little in the way of evening entertainment and just a few local excursions. Guests slip quickly into the slow pace of things and seem to relish the art of pottering from the room to the beach to the restaurant to the bar to the spa to the room again. The Angsana Spa is award-winning and wonderful.

To raise the heartbeat there is some excellent diving to be had in this still untouched atoll (shared with just one other resort). Ocean Pro run an impressive set up with excellent information displays and a wide choice of diving options, to entice the guests to make this a part of their daily or weekly plan. The 32 sites are documented with laminated maps, descriptions, boat trip time and star system for corals, big fish, current and difficulty. Up to three dives a day are possible either from the resort or during their full-day trips and a number of speciality courses are always available. The base is popular with experienced repeaters (internet pre-booking is encouraged and some divers even leave their equipment behind for their return) while, for absolute beginners, the lagoon directly in front of the base is an ideal spot for courses.

Some snorkeling is to be had around the corals in the eastern lagoon, the ocean-facing side, but there is no access through to the drop-off. Consequently the resort sends out a free boat twice a day to this housereef and offers a paying trip three times a week to another local spot. The western, lagoon-facing side is good for trying out some windsurfing or swimming around, as it deepens quickly and the floor is clear and sandy.

The main restaurant and bar are next to each other on the lagoon side. With a wide beach here, they are beautifully positioned for drinks on the beach and candlelit dinners on the waterfront. Thatched over wood frames, open-sided and with sand on the floor, they are both attractive and relaxed.

Now with top-class cuisine, modern rooms and a fine spa, a great resort just got even better.

1	2	**3**	4	5	6	7	8	9	10
LOWEST		RELATIVE PRICE			HIGHEST				

1	2	3	**4**	5	6	7	8	9	10
MOST			ROOM DENSITY				LEAST		

T 664 5051   F 664 0176
E info@asdu.com
www.asdu.com

North Male Atoll

95 mins

 $3

 $2

 $3

1/2 $15

 $15

 Sub Maldive

 $56

6 x $264

PADI $360

Asdu Sun Island

Asdu is a relic of the original Maldives. It is really a hidden gem of a resort, even if it is unpolished.

As every other resort has been reconstructed and upgraded, this one alone has remained unchanged.

It is hidden in the sense of feeling isolated, having only two islands on its horizon (Dhiffushi and Meeru). It is also hidden in the sense that the resort never advertises and doesn't show up at trade fairs or join trade associations.

Word of mouth is the best advertising and Asdu continues to thrive on this alone. Italians are the majority guests, combining with a mix of other Europeans, and probably half of all guests book directly with Ahmed Ismail, the genial Maldivian who owns, runs and lives on the island, with his wife and son.

On this very small island there are just 30 rooms and a single reception, bar and restaurant building. There is no second restaurant or coffee shop, no tv or karaoke lounge, no swimming pool or tennis court. This is a place to come when you want to leave the modern world back in Europe and live the simple life for a while.

All the rooms are just a few metres from the lagoon and all are similarly simple. Built in blocks of two or three, they have a telephone but no hot water or air conditioning. They are slightly higher and larger than most rooms, so enabling the slatted windows and latticed space below the roof to keep the sun out but let any breeze through. It is a practical and stylish design using local wood, coir rope and screw-pine matting. Unfortunately from the outside they are not attractive, as the rooms have corrugated sheet roofs.

The central building too has a painted corrugated sheet roof and painted concrete floors and patio. It is not a naturally beautiful island either, with scrubby vegetation and few large palms, but somehow the unusual magic of the place works its way into your bones and you remember only the enjoyment of simple pleasures.

The simplest pleasure of all is friendship and good conversation. With a small number of like-minded guests, often professionals, and a genial host family, there is plenty of easy interaction between the guests. The atmosphere is calm and sophisticated.

The other simple pleasures are the beach and the lagoon. Islands inside atolls tend to have smaller lagoons and better beaches than those on the outside, and this is no exception. The beaches from the west to the south are good to very good, though it must be said that the rooms on the north side of the island now have only intermittent beaches at best.

The lagoon, sandy and neither too deep nor too shallow, is ideal for swimming. The reef drop-off, extensive and never far away, is excellent for snorkeling. This is certainly one of the highlights and, in some ways, a reward for not undergoing reconstruction or pumping sand from the lagoon. So many resort reefs have suffered from this but not Asdu.

The dive base is small and not very busy but it is very reasonably priced. The diving in the region is first class, with a mix of local thilas and channels on the eastern rim of the atoll, above Meeru. There isn't much in the way of watersports but the kayaks are free and the windsurfers are cheap (and often free too).

Drinks are very well priced. And any laundry is done for free. This just isn't the sort of place that will sting you for extras, quite the opposite in fact.

All the meals are set. It is not gourmet stuff, but it is at least good, tasty fare based around a lot of fresh fish caught that day (usually by your waiter or another member of staff).

Asdu continues to live its own life, independent of the fashionable changes that all the other resorts undergo (whether successful or not). For a taste of the original Maldives Asdu now has no competition. For many clients this is nothing to boast about, but for others there is a special magic that needs to be experienced to be understood.

| 1 | 2 | 3 | 4 | **5** | 6 | 7 | 8 | 9 | 10 | | 1 | 2 | 3 | **4** | 5 | 6 | 7 | 8 | 9 | 10 |

LOWEST   RELATIVE PRICE   HIGHEST   MOST   ROOM DENSITY   LEAST

T 668 0508 F 668 0574
E admin@athuruga.com.mv
www.planhotel.ch

South Ari Atoll

 25 mins

inc

inc

inc

$30

$15

The Crab

$76

6 x $422

PADI $720

Athuruga

For an all-inclusive resort it is very hard to beat either Athuruga or its sister island and neighbour, Thudufushi.

Here they really do it properly: no compromises on quality and just about everything available free at any time. That includes the minibar, premium brand drinks, cappuccinos, ice cream, fresh snacks and even cigarettes and sun cream. There is a sense that you have temporarily joined a rather smart club where money isn't mentioned. And when a liveried young man appears beside you, once more offering a chilled face towel at just the right moment, you know it has to be true.

Like any good club, the members are loyal and it's not always easy to get in. With a solid core of repeaters and a great word-of-mouth reputation, Athuruga regularly wins the national award for highest occupancy in its category ('less than 50 rooms'). Apart from the service and value aspects, it's a neat little island with a quite exceptional level of maintenance. The resort was built in 1990 but looks now just as smart as it did then.

The downside for some would be that on such a small island the many buildings rather squeeze the space, and their style is of the 'solid', formal type. This, however, suits the clientele who are a little older on average and who like to dress up a bit in the evenings.

A stroll after dinner around the substantial, and very attractive, shopping arcade would be just the place to pick up some appropriate clothing. Alongside the Italian-run boutique is a tailor's, with a selection of material, and a jeweller's, as well as the usual souvenir and casual-wear shop, a dive shop, a 'drug store' and an infirmary.

Every evening there is some form of entertainment put on or organised by the European members of staff: musical favourites before and after dinner, a short cabaret, floodlit volleyball etc. This is perhaps enjoyed most by the Italians who make up 30% of the guests, but is by no means avoided by the remaining German (60%) and British guests. In any case, however far down the beach you settle for a drink, you will always be reached and served. Nothing is too much trouble.

"We never say no", is how the headwaiter put it. "For example, dinner is served on the beach for anniversaries, birthdays and departure nights, but also for anyone who requests it. Recently, one couple had all 28 nights outside the restaurant."

Another example is the dive system, which couldn't be easier on the guests. Once you've signed up for a dive, your equipment is taken to the boat for you. After the dive you just walk away, while the equipment is returned, rinsed and shelved by the dive base staff. Having said that, the level of information on the dive sites (location, topography, fish) is not so impressive. And being in the middle of the atoll means longer journeys to the outside channels. On the other hand, great thilas such as Orimas and Fish Head are all regular dives.

Snorkeling is excellent here, with lots to see and a housereef that is always accessible. Although at one point it expands away from the island, creating a sizeable lagoon, there are four channels cut through to give you a choice of how far you go. Snorkeling trips to nearby thilas and a sandbank are arranged with the watersports centre, which run all the excursions in a personalised way. A comfortable speedboat and flexible staff make for numerous possibilities.

The 46 rooms are ideally placed around the circumference of the island, with views and immediate access to the water but with some shade directly in front. Eight rooms are individual, the remainder are in pairs. An additional row of five rooms are tucked in behind, for overbooking periods. All the rooms are identical: solid and pristine. From the half open-air bathroom, with double basins and bidet, through the fair-sized bedrooms, with telling details like wooden clothes hangers and dressing gowns, out to the timber-decked verandah with its two wicker easy chairs, it is clear that no corners are being cut here. This is an island where the customer is king and he gets real value for money. But no need to mention money.

1	2	3	4	**5**	6	7	8	9	10
LOWEST		RELATIVE PRICE		HIGHEST					

1	2	3	4	**5**	6	7	8	9	10
MOST			ROOM DENSITY			LEAST			

T 664 0088 F 664 3877
E sales@bandos.com.mv
www.bandos.com

North Male Atoll

 20 mins

$5

$2

$4

1/2 $20

$26

Dive Bandos

$63

6 x $363

PADI $657

Bandos

Bandos has long been a popular choice for an active, pro-family resort close to Male, with good snorkeling and diving.

Reopened in 2005 after a major upgrade, it is still all those things but with an added layer of fine accommodation and extra facilities. The look and feel is a balance between the formal and the casual.

This balance is symbolised by the thatched roofs on every building contrasting with the tiles on every floor. It is an informal island but not always a barefoot island. It has an internet hotspot and large plasma tv, as well as a conference hall, near to the reception, but it still has its tranquil verandahs, tall palms and pockets of private beach.

Families are not just welcome here but catered for. In the interior is a large sports centre with tennis, badminton, squash, table tennis, gym and table games (as well as massage, sauna and steam rooms). For the much younger children there is a childcare room with appropriate toys and an outdoor play area. Female staff members are on hand to look after the children and are available for babysitting in the evenings.

There is good shade at the water's edge, which is essential, but many rooms don't have much beach and the lagoon tends to deepen quite quickly. Children who are neither very young nor old enough for the big games might well find other children around to play with, as this is one of the largest resort islands in terms of size and number of rooms. Some rooms in the first two categories have the interconnecting door that makes a family room.

The Standard Rooms (84 beach front, 19 non-beach front) alternate between a twin and double bed set-up (ideal for family rooms). Fresh and new, like all the rooms, they have pleasant green and gold furnishings, stone effect floor tiles and a small sitting area partitioned off by a balcony. The bathroom is small but the shower is good. Those that face sunset (the early numbers) also have the good fortune of one of the best sections of beach.

The 48 Junior Suites are arranged in closes, or arcs, of rooms with a shared garden in front. The beach in this section almost disappears at high tide, sadly, but the room interiors offer some compensation. The two-tone yellow and ochre scheme of the sitting room, the solid wood four-poster with its oatmeal drapes and the overall sense of light, style and privacy definitely lift the spirits. Tea and coffee facilities are always welcome, the tv is best (almost only) seen from the bed, and the white tiled floor gets a bit cold under the a/c.

Of the 24 Garden Villas inside the island, 12 are in a line along the side of the new swimming pool (these may well become known as Pool Villas). Not as large as the Junior Suites, they are darker, cosier and have a hint of the East in their decor. Within a short walk of a good beach, their main selling point is the proximity to the pool, with its wide deck, sunloungers and swim-up bar.

The 48 Beach Villas are the last and greatest of the land rooms to be built. Once the gardens in front of the rooms (in closes) have grown up again the lovely picture will be complete. Each room is a double-storey, circular building with the bedroom upstairs and a little balcony looking out to sea. From the wooden floorboards to the deep orange paint that offsets the earthy colours, these are rooms that give you that little superior feeling. The bathroom only adds to it: half inside and half out, its fittings are very modern and attractive, all the way out to the thatched jacuzzi.

The last half of the beach villas have good beach outside but, on the whole, this is one area that is disappointing. The snorkeling, however, is still good and always close by. One can snorkel all the way around the island or come in via one of the three cut-throughs.

The dive base is large and impressive. It seems to offer everything from absolute beginner courses up to expert rebreather courses. It is a PADI Gold Palm Resort and a Platinum Facility of the International Association of Nitrox and Technical Divers. To cap it all, it has one of the only decompression chambers in the country.

The main restaurant delivers three decent buffets a day though the place itself is rather dark and dull. The fine dining restaurant has sea views but is none too attractive either. The coffee shop and main bar are well placed by the water. The bar is the main focus of nighttime entertainment and this is usually active and buzzing till sometimes very late indeed.

All in all, the upgrading is making the regular Bandos guests very happy. It is the same casual Bandos with that added layer of modern style and facilities.

| 1 | 2 | 3 | 4 | 5 | 6 | 7 | **8** | 9 | 10 | | 1 | 2 | 3 | **4** | 5 | 6 | 7 | 8 | 9 | 10 |

LOWEST   RELATIVE PRICE   HIGHEST   MOST   ROOM DENSITY   LEAST

T 664 3147 F 664 3843
E maldives@banyantree.com
www.banyantree.com

Images down right side courtesy of Banyan Tree

North Male Atoll

25 mins

$6

$6

$7

1/2 $35

$25

Marine
Centre

$85

6 x $480

PADI $655

Banyan Tree

Banyan Tree is an upscale resort for couples who prioritise privacy, peacefulness and a renowned spa.

Honeymoons and wedding vow renewals are understandably popular here. However it is also a resort that has gained respect and popularity for its green credentials, particularly its work with turtles, sharks and coral regeneration.

The island, called Vabbinfaru, is conveniently located near enough to the airport for quick transfers yet far enough to be well away from any traffic and so undisturbed by sight or sound. Like many islands inside the atolls, including its neighbour and sister resort Angsana, it is small, roughly circular, has a close housereef and very good beaches.

The best beach faces west and as that is also the direction of the afternoon sun and sunset this is where most of the more expensive rooms are. Aside from the top Vabbinfaru Villa, the 48 rooms are divided between Beach Front Villas and Deluxe Beach Front Villas, which are on the beach, and Ocean View Villas and Deluxe Ocean View Villas, which are tucked behind those rooms. Some of the deluxe rooms of both categories face the sunrise, while the regular rooms face north.

All the rooms are the same size but the deluxe rooms use some finer materials. All electricity goes off when the card key is removed from its slot and the a/c must be separately restarted. The best plan is probably to throw the doors open and enjoy the inside/outside life for which the rooms are well designed. The relatively small rooms then spill out onto a fair sized deck and then a garden for the Ocean View Villas or the beach for the Beach Front Villas. Each room has a jacuzzi and also a 'sala' or pavilion, which is inside the attractive, private gardens or, for the beach villas, at the end of a covered walkway out over the beach.

The beach salas tend to reduce the amount of walking around the outside of the island and that increases the privacy although, for a five-star resort, the relatively large number of rooms to island size means being sometimes aware of your sunbathing neighbours on the beach.

Banyan Tree brings a Southeast Asian look and feel to the resort that works very well. All the buildings are made from Indonesian materials, down to the thatch on the roofs. The spa is where it works best of all. Its reception is a little straight-edged and formal but the treatment rooms are large and lovely. And the highly trained Thai and Balinese therapists are so good that the spa often becomes a major part of the guests' holiday even if that wasn't their original intention.

Beyond the traditional massages, the spa offers seductive combinations of treatments, including facials, scrubs, rainmist showers, acupressure and much more that build into two and three-hour sessions. There is even a seven-hour full day session that works through your body from top to toe.

Sited next to the dive base, the spa offers special treatments discounted for divers. Diving is set at one double-tank dive a day, which is less active than most dive centres but, having said that, the attached Marine Centre is constantly active in a range of valuable projects. Having begun with tracking coral regrowth after the 1998 bleaching event, it moved on to studying methods of encouraging that regrowth. It then began research on sharks, both purely scientific and around their economic value. But its most visible and popular work has been with the endangered Green Sea Turtles. A small number of eggs are raised on the island for 12-18 months and then released with a tag and, in a few instances, a satellite transmitter. Turtles are probably second only to dolphins in the affections of visitors to Maldives, so seeing them in all sizes swimming happily around the lagoon is a real bonus for visitors to this resort.

The final highlight of the resort is the food. Lunch is a quite wonderful selection spread out in the shade beside the beach. Dinner is an excellent set menu with enough choice to make everyone happy. Alternative dinner venues include a sandbank for two, with water lapping around your feet.

T 664 2672 F 664 3497
E info@baros.com.mv
www.universalresorts.com

1	2	3	4	5	6	**7**	8	9	10
LOWEST			RELATIVE PRICE			HIGHEST			

1	2	3	4	5	6	7	8	9	10
MOST			ROOM DENSITY					LEAST	

All images except aerial courtesy of Baros

North Male Atoll

 20 mins

 50 mins

 $5.50

 $5.50

 $3.85

1/2 $50

 $35

Baros International

 $67

6 x $368

PADI $623

Baros

The new Baros is clearly a labour of love. Something special and something new to Maldives has been imagined and brought to fruition.

Baros is one of those resorts that has built up a devoted following of repeat visitors. It was closed down in 2005, rebuilt and then re-opened as something entirely new and different. Well, maybe not so different. It has managed to retain the essential intimacy, friendliness and closeness to nature that people so loved about Baros. But the radical changes of build, style and service now place the resort among the élite.

With each aspect of the resort designed as an 'event' to draw out more pleasure, Baros leaves guests with even deeper impressions than before. Impressions that linger even longer in the memory.

Walking down the jetty for the first time, one's eyes are drawn to the beautiful lines of the restaurants built into the lagoon. Combined with entering the grand reception, impressive yet not overstated, guests get an immediate and satisfying sense of arrival. Or even, as they say of owning a luxury car, of having arrived.

This impression is enriched when guests get to their room and look around. The quality of the workmanship is obvious; the style is modern and a touch 'different'. There are three categories, the Deluxe Villas (24), the Baros Villas (20) and the Water Villas (30) - not including the one Pool Villa. The Deluxe Villas are elegant and relatively simple (without a four-poster). The other categories give you the feeling of walking into a coffee table book of chic hotel rooms. The designer fittings, the brilliantly concealed television and DVD player, the Pininfarina coffee maker and the well-stocked wine cooler tell you that a great deal of thought and attention has gone into making the rooms a significant part of your holiday.

When I tell you that every room is just a few feet away from the beach or the lagoon and each has a very large deck with a bolstered daybed and a dining table, then you won't be surprised to read that a large portion of guests are not seen anywhere else on the resort for days on end. As the wines in the cooler are very well priced and room service is 24 hours a day, it makes 'staying at home' a most enticing option.

In fact it is the food and wine even more than the beautiful setting that secures Baros's place among the élite resorts. The Lighthouse Restaurant is the one building that is not thatched, but it has a dramatic white peaked roof that marks it out as the icon of the resort. Upstairs is a classy lounge bar with panoramic views, which is just the place for a pre-prandial martini cocktail or glass of champagne. Downstairs is one of the true haute cuisine restaurants in the country, serving an eclectic menu of Asian and Mediterranean classics and fusions. Not only is the wine cellar extensive but renowned wine growers are invited to present and talk about their vintages.

The second restaurant of note is the Cayenne Grill where seafood, meat and vegetarian dishes are prepared in your choice of eight distinct styles and served at your own thatched pavilion on decking beside the water's edge. The Lime Restaurant is the all-day and more informal dining option. As everyone comes on a bed and breakfast arrangement these restaurants, as well as the villa dining, are critical to the resort's success and reputation.

The usual factors that build a resort's reputation have always been here. Snorkeling is good and access is very good, as the reef runs close around most of the island. The beach surrounds the island and is mostly excellent with just a small area of less fine sand in front of some deluxe rooms. A low wall in the lagoon has been deemed necessary in order to protect the beach from erosion.

The island is still an example of Maldivian nature at its best. The following years will see the replanted plants and flowers blossom to their original glory around the public areas and in front of those few deluxe rooms that lack complete shade and privacy.

The final critical factor is the quality of the staff, and Baros is admirably served by new top professionals, as well as others who have stayed with the resort year after year, much to the returning guests' delight.

| | | | | | | | | | | | | | | | | | | | | |
| 1 | 2 | 3 | **4** | 5 | 6 | 7 | 8 | 9 | 10 | | **1** | 2 | 3 | 4 | 5 | 6 | 7 | 8 | 9 | 10 |

LOWEST   RELATIVE PRICE   HIGHEST   MOST   ROOM DENSITY   LEAST

T 664 3517 F 664 5924
E gateway@dhivehinet.net.mv
www.bolifushi.com

South Male Atoll

 30 mins

70 mins

 $3.30

 $3.30

 $4.40

1/2 $28

 $17

 Bolifushi

 $50

5 x $240

PADI $480

Bolifushi

Bolifushi is a small, pretty island near Male, with good snorkeling, a fine lagoon and excellent beaches.

It is also one of those islands that mixes a large majority of Italian club holidaymakers with a minority of German, Swiss and Japanese quiet holiday seekers. Sometimes this works out fine and sometimes neither party quite get what they have come for.

The layout of the island is simple. Coming down the arrival jetty the guest faces a beautifully neat, ornamental display of sculptured bushes and tidy thatch over white coral walls. Here are the public buildings of the reception, restaurant, coffee shop and bar, as well as the spa, which occupies the first two of the 'Boli rooms'. These Boli rooms are the standard rooms that arc around the north side of the island, facing the main action beach and the waterbungalows. The quiet beach is on the next side (the west and northwest sides), where the Beach Villas are. The dive school and watersports centre take up the next part of the island and then it's back down past the restaurant again.

It takes just a few minutes to stroll around the place but if you go on the beach it takes a lot longer because this is A grade, softest, deepest sand. The few groynes with large round ends are like features of the resort and none of them hinder views from the rooms or direct access to the beach.

The snorkeling is either between the over-water coffee shop and waterbungalows or around the west side (in front of the beach villas). A channel makes the west side more rewarding but also trickier as the current is sometimes strong. Most people stick to the easier section, which is still good, especially for coral regrowth.

A couple of sunken boats add to the quality of house-reef diving but generally the trips need to go either to the other side of the atoll or up to the southern end of North Male Atoll, where there are a number of well-known Protected Marine Areas. The instructors speak Italian, Japanese and English but not much German or Russian. The lagoon, which is soft and only gradually goes down, is ideal for lessons.

The dive and watersports participation has declined with the arrival of Veratour, whose accent is more on guests having fun on the beach during the day, in the bar at night and out on excursions together. (That should mean, of course, more personalised attention for those who do want to do diving and watersports).

In other parts of the world Veratour do a full-on energetic and noisy good time but here that style is carefully restricted. For example, the aqua aerobics is the quietest I have seen and nothing must take place after 11.15 at night, except the once-a-week live band. The other evening entertainments are an underwater video, a magic show, a cabaret and a big quiz. All of this happens in the over-water bar and coffee shop (with its large decking area outside). This is a fine spot for it all, but there isn't an alternative 'quiet bar'.

The Italian guides and animators do a fine job with their clients, keeping them well informed and entertained. The other guests are left pretty much to their own devices, with information on a board in the reception.

The 15 Waterbungalows are, as usual, the premium rooms. On a triangular jetty, they face north, east and west. The decking is a fair size but you do see everyone on your side. The interior is smart but rather dim, with their dark wood floors and walls. There is an espresso maker and kettle for tea and a large television, which just shows the news channels.

The Beach Villas share the same interior as the Waterbungalows except for white walls and a bathtub but no espresso maker. Their decks are on stilts with a view of good beaches, but their privacy is not the best and the wooden sunloungers don't have a cover.

The Boli rooms are simple, clean and unpretentious. They are not large but they have what you need (air-conditioning, a powerful shower and a hairdryer) and open directly out to the large, 'all-together' beach.

Image above and image below courtesy of Amridesign

North Male Atoll

 15 mins

 35 mins

 inc

 inc

 inc

 $40

 $15

 Ocean Venture

 $60

5 x $300

PADI $524

Club Faru

From the people who run Fihalhohi comes this new all-inclusive resort, taking over the beautiful structures that were left behind by the departing Club Med.

A ten-minute boat ride from the airport brings you not to the end of a long jetty but to the landing platform, which is a part of the main public area. Surrounding the broad deck of a fine swimming pool stand separate pavilions, with red earth tiled roofs and ornately worked wood supports, like something out of Old China.

The reception building connected to the restaurant sets the backdrop. To one side of the pool is the light and airy main bar, on the other side is the games room pavilion, with television, pool table, table football and table tennis. With excursions heading out from the arrival platform, this is where most of the action happens during the day. Having said that, Club Faru (despite its name) is a quiet place for people looking to relax and do their own thing in their own time.

Then again, there are some guests here that want a bit of fun and activity and they are also catered for. On the southern end of the island, where the sun shines all day on a large bulge of beach, there are daytime activities such as volleyball, badminton and watersports. Canoes and kayaks are free to use and the sail and powered sports are reasonably priced.

An animator organises events during the day and is involved in the evening entertainments that happen at this end too, in the large, ornate coffee shop and à la carte restaurant. Live bands come twice a week and on other nights there are karaoke sessions and discos as well as short cabaret sessions.

The 152 rooms are in nicely designed two-storey blocks and are all the same except for the fact that the upper storey rooms don't have the third bed that is built into the downstairs rooms. An archway takes you into the large, tiled verandah with built-in cushioned seating.

Inside, the rooms have a double arched roof, rounded walls and circular windows. It is always a pleasure to see the rectangle altered and these are lovely clean and cosy rooms. The bathrooms are small and functional compared with how they are in so many resorts nowadays, but they're OK.

The first five blocks of rooms have good shade and a fine broad beach in front of them and face west to the sunset. These are clearly the best rooms to go for. The blocks further down the west side have distinctly less beach and some seagrass in the shady, shallow lagoon until the beach opens out again at the southern bulge. Just under half the rooms are on the other side, the quiet eastern side, where the beach goes from excellent to narrow. It should be said, however, that some of those rooms and the whole of the southern beach look out to Hulhumale, which is the man-made extension of the airport island that is destined to become a new town.

The lagoon is good for watersports, being large, shallow and sandy, but no good for snorkeling as the reef is inaccessible and there is little coral inside the lagoon. The resort, however, puts on two snorkeling trips a day to a nearby reef and these are free for all guests. (Guests also get a free tour of Male.) Diving in the region is long established and rather well worn but still there are good things to be seen in the channels and outside reefs of North Male Atoll. I saw my only whale shark to date on the outside reef of this island.

For a quiet, all-inclusive resort that has a bit of action when you want it Club Faru might just work for you. If you get one of the best-located rooms and spend your days on the beach and around the lovely public area, it should definitely work for you. Being so close to Male has its advantages too, as well as some disadvantages.

1 2 3 4 5 **6** 7 8 9 10   1 2 **3** 4 5 6 7 8 9 10

LOWEST   RELATIVE PRICE   HIGHEST   MOST   ROOM DENSITY   LEAST

T 664 3152 F 664 4859
E reckan@clubmed-rani.com.mv
www.clubmed.com

All images below courtesy of Club Med

North Male Atoll

 30 mins

 inc

 inc

 inc

1/2 $85

 Eurodivers

 $53

5 x $250

PADI $531

Club Med Kani

Club Med is not what it used to be. Kani, like all its Asian properties, is now five-star (or 'four tritons').

It looks and feels like one of the top ranking resorts, yet its original values - those things that made Club Med Club Med - are still at the heart of the place.

This is the most active resort, with the most entertainment in the country. You probably could have a quiet holiday in a distant waterbungalow but that's not the point. Here the watersports and snorkeling equipment is free and so are the lessons. There are daily tournaments in volleyball, football, table tennis, badminton and petanque. A tennis court should replace the basketball court at some point.

The key thing is there isn't a "rah rah, let's go!" atmosphere. It is altogether more mature and sophisticated, where everyone knows what is going on and they can take it or leave it. For example, there are five types of fitness classes each day but just a handful of committed participants. Most guests, however, do participate in the daytime animation at the poolside and enjoy the showtime at the main bar in the evening, followed by dancing into the night.

It is the staff who bring the Club Med feel to the island. When not mixing with the guests or performing in front of them, they are hidden away practising for another show. Multinational, with a large contingent of Europeans, they bring a freshness and enthusiasm which is catching and distinctively Club Med. As for the guests, up to half are French, a significant number are Italian and Japanese and the remainder are a mix of Asian nationalities and British.

Both Asian and European cuisine feature at every buffet. And every buffet is spectacular. Cuisine has long been one of Club Med's strengths and as this resort moved upmarket the variety and quality of the food just moved even higher. No wonder there is an emphasis on sport and exercise!

The land rooms come in two categories: 120 Superior and 20 Beach Villas. The Beach Villas are somewhat larger and have better locations but otherwise they share the same good quality furniture, interior decoration and lighting. One simply doesn't spend much time in the room on a resort such as this.

You would, however, be tempted to stay around longer in one of the 75 Lagoon Suites. These are large and elegant, with a 'visitor's room', the high-ceilinged bedroom overlooking a broad wooden deck and a beautifully designed bathroom. The best located suites have delightful views to open sea but others will look out to a nearby inhabited island.

The lagoon, not too deep and with a sandy floor, is ideal for playing in and swimming. It is too large to reach any snorkeling reef but there are two free snorkeling trips a day and free equipment provided. Diving is well established in the region and popular on the resort.

One side of the island faces into the atoll and the other side faces out to the ocean. This means the atoll facing side has a fine beach and there is difficulty retaining a beach on the ocean side. One advantage is that it is much quieter away from all the activities on 'the front', but there is an added disadvantage of a very close new island in the lagoon that is far from attractive. On the other hand, there are only a few rooms that are really affected by this.

Finally, in the midst of all the unhurried activity is a dreamy spa straight out of Bali. Enclosed in a verdant garden of tropical flowers are individual pavilions made from coconut wood columns and cotton walls. The atmosphere is hushed, incense drifts on the breeze and Balinese therapists await to ease those ... what? Well, you'll think of some excuse to keep coming back.

Club Med is now a very classy resort yet still draws on its heritage of fun, sports and showtime.

| 1 | 2 | 3 | 4 | 5 | 6 | 7 | 8 | **9** | 10 | | 1 | 2 | 3 | **4** | 5 | 6 | 7 | 8 | 9 | 10 |
| LOWEST | | | RELATIVE PRICE | | | | HIGHEST | | | | MOST | | | | ROOM DENSITY | | | | LEAST | |

T 664 1818 F 664 1919
E sales@cocoa-island.com.mv
www.cocoa-island.com

Images above courtesy of Cocoa Island

South Male Atoll

10 mins

45 mins

$6

$7 (1ltr)

$5

1/2 $100

$35

Ocean Paradise

$71

5 x $355

PADI $646

Cocoa Island

Of the growing number of international five-star resorts, Cocoa remains the smallest, in size and number of rooms.

The quietness of the place is not just relaxing, it is serene, due, in part, to an exceptional openness of design which offers deep seascapes or intimate landscapes from wherever you may be. Serenity and well-being are the keys to the place, and ever more so with the developing influence of the 'Shambhala Retreat'.

There are no walls to the reception. You sit amid antique South Asian furniture and look out to patterns of light and shade, a dappled green canopy above white coral sand. There is only a back wall to the restaurant and to the bar. Between the wooden pillars the views are all shades of blue, across the infinity pool to the lagoon and the channel beyond.

The rooms are not open-sided but seem that way. Of the four categories, the 2 Two Bedroom Villas, the 4 One Bedroom Villas and the 12 Dhoni Loft Suites have full-length windows on three sides. The 18 Dhoni Suites have just the one side so designed though light still pervades the room, bouncing off the white painted timber walls, off-white upholstery and wheat coloured carpet. Dark wooden furniture, South Asian and colonial in style, balance the effect.

The differences between a Dhoni Suite and a Dhoni Loft Suite are a high ceiling, a loft for the bedroom and a floor area almost half as big again. The Dhoni Suites may have king-size or twin beds whereas the Loft Suites only have king-size beds. Strung along a curving walkway both types of rooms have good privacy. Immediate neighbours are hidden but rooms further down the line are visible. The One Bedroom Villas have screens in the water ensuring complete privacy and the Two Bedroom Villas are positioned at the very tips of the walkway, looking out to an uninterrupted horizon (one facing the sunrise, the other the sunset).

One can swim to the lagoon drop-off from all but two of the rooms. The fish life is very good, but coral regrowth is disappointing. Low tide is very low, prohibiting direct access to the reef, or even swimming for a while. Access is then from a jetty at one end of the Suites and a cut-through at the other. Alternatively it could be time to check the snorkeling on the other side of the island. Here the drop-off is more precipitous and the fish life at least as good, with the largest trumpet fish I have ever seen, as well as sharks, turtles and pelagics passing through.

As there are no rooms on the island itself (all are waterbungalows), there has been no need to build groynes to try to hold onto the shifting sand. The result is an island closer to its original state, with long tapering beaches at each end. However, at low tide it becomes clear that the long walkways have to some extent impeded the flow of sand from one end to the other. Then again, with no dredging to fill gaps, the quality of the beaches remains excellent.

The island is neatly split into three parts. The middle part has the reception, the unimpressive dive and watersports centres and the service area. This leaves the sunrise end and its beach to the Shambhala Retreat and the sunset end and its beach to the restaurant, bar and swimming pool.

This latter leisure area looks as smart as it is relaxed. There is an easy flow between external and internal spaces. The food is terrific, even for this standard of resort. With an emphasis on fresh fish and seafood, an outstanding Australian chef blends and develops Indian and Sri Lankan traditions, alongside familiar and less familiar Western dishes.

There is also an accent on healthy eating which echoes Cocoa Island's underlying philosophy of well-being. In the same way, the Shambhala Retreat is at the heart of the resort, however rarely or frequently it is visited.

Many spas on Maldives resorts, it must be said, are squeezed in as an afterthought, as one more facility on offer. Here it is clearly thought through, from its location to its treatments and its wider goals. The company has a sister spa, the Shambhala at Parrot Key on Turks and Caicos, which was once voted 'best spa in the world'. The Shambhala on Cocoa will surely develop in significance and wider reputation.

Set around an open courtyard of fine white sand, under the shade of indigenous trees and palms, the treatment rooms can be air-conditioned or opened out to the breezes and sounds of lapping water. Ayurvedic therapy is offered alongside massage therapy with the same aims of relieving tension, calming the mind and rejuvenating the body. The therapists are exceptionally good.

Vaavu Atoll

- 35 mins
- 100 mins
- $3.50/inc
- $3.50/inc
- inc
- $31
- $17
- Dhiggiri
- $53
- 5 x $260
- PADI $533

Dhiggiri

This is a delightful resort. Small, pretty and attractively designed in the original Maldives style, it also boasts easy access to all-round snorkeling, luxury diving and good beaches.

I would like to write that it is a total relaxation place, which it is - and it isn't. 60% of the guests are Italian (through Franco Rosso) and their days are filled with collective activities, from aqua gym to table tennis tournaments and salsa dancing through to evening cabarets and live 'piano bar' music. In between there are the excursions and snorkeling trips. This is all relaxation to the Italian guest. The German and British guests, on the other hand, usually prefer to sip drinks, lay back and do very little, in between the odd dive and excursion.

On other islands this contest of relaxation versus 'club' doesn't work but for a combination of reasons it does work here. Crucially, the staff and management are attentive, active and flexible. Responding to the different groups that arrive, everything is done to make sure everyone gets just what they are looking for. And most of the time that is just how it pans out. A key indication of this success is the exceptionally high rate of return guests, year after year.

The resort is entirely all-inclusive. Not only are canoes and windsurfers free but initial lessons are too. Snorkeling equipment is included and so are one fisherman's island trip and one sunset cruise with cocktails. In fact, a whole range of cocktails is free on demand up to midnight - from Caiparinas to Negronis.

A bonus for fellow guests is the quality of the food demanded by the Italian guests. It is not at all exclusively Italian, there are many dishes designed for the Germans and British, but it is all well prepared and as fresh as possible. Not every meal is a buffet, five evening meals are set, which I often prefer. A choice of plates served at your table is a nice change of pace and is always a 'unified' cuisine instead of yet another mixed up buffet.

The housereef snorkeling is good, but one should be careful with the currents as this island sits right in the middle of Dhiggiri Channel. Of course, the strong current attracts lots of different fish, including the big predators. The reef drop-off is no more than twenty-five metres away most of the way around the island. In addition, there are guided snorkeling trips every morning and afternoon.

With this one small and just one other medium sized resort (Alimatha) in the atoll, the dive sites are still pristine and you'll rarely see another boat near your destination. The many channels offer great diving and though it can be challenging in the strong currents that sometimes prevail, the staff at the dive school are experienced and very safety conscious. Certainly their service is second to none. The diver has only to sign his or her room number onto a list and walk away. Everything is then taken care of by the staff, from the preparation of the equipment to the washing and hanging up after the dive.

There are just 45 rooms here - 20 Water-bungalows (taken by Franco Rosso) and 25 Beach Bungalows. Both room interiors are essentially the same and very attractive, with their weathered, antique look, four-poster bed and curvy lines. The first few waterbungalows can see both sunrise and sunset, while the last few are just a few metres away from the reef drop-off. The beach bungalows are still the beautiful old coral rondavels and every one of them, indeed every building on the island, is thatched.

The western tip has a fine tongue of sand snaking into the lagoon that attracts more guests, while the quiet south side has a series of large groynes with rounded ends doubling as sunbathing spots. All the rooms have at least some beach in front of them (except the waterbungalows of course) and the view is unimpeded by bushes or trees.

Altogether this resort looks good and feels great. It is run calmly and casually to make two types of holidays perfectly possible in the same place.

T 666 0751 F 666 0727
E info@dhonimighili.com
www.dhonimighili.com

All images except aerial courtesy of Dhoni Mighili

North Ari Atoll

 30 mins

 inc

 inc

 inc

 Divers Haven

 $130

3 x $275

PADI $900

Dhoni Mighili

Dhoni Mighili is in a class of its own. That's because it alone is classified as a picnic island - but also because no other resort offers such a chance to design and live your own fantasy holiday.

The main reason for this is that the 'rooms' are actually boats and there are just six of them. Each couple in each boat has a butler, a captain and two crew whose only job is to look after their wishes and whims. Yet the freedom to travel anywhere at anytime is only half the story. The six boats are matched by six rooms on an island with beautiful beaches, a wonderful spa and a host and hostess who are sophisticated, entertaining and organised.

Waking up in your island room, you stroll to breakfast barefooted in deep fine sand, perhaps wearing one of the complimentary sarongs. With the sand spread throughout the bar, lounge and restaurant there is no need to put your footwear back on. And there is no need to turn up on time, as there is no on time. Any meal is arranged, anywhere, with a word to your butler.

Your butler - or thakuru as he is called - is your right-hand man who not only makes things happen but also suggests ideas for the day's activities and meals. Slipping anchor and cruising away under sail or motor you might snorkel in the morning, have lunch served on a desert island, sunbathe, then visit an inhabited island or two in the afternoon before putering back at sunset through a channel frequented by dolphins.

The variations on this theme of slacking in paradise are myriad and limited only by the hours of daylight, for the boats return to base every evening. In that time the hundreds of islands and hidden reefs of Ari Atoll are all within reach. So too is the hammerhead shark point on Rasdhoo Atoll. For diving, the instructor simply comes on board with the equipment and dives with you. However, you don't have to go far for highlights. Truly prime snorkeling is available on neighbouring Kandholhudhoo island that somehow, astonishingly, was untouched by the coral bleaching event of 1998.

The sea is calm for most of the year and like glass for much of the high season. Only at the turn of the seasons is it choppy and rainy - that's May/June and November. So life onboard is almost always serene, private and luxurious.

The king-size bed has Frette linen and a goose down duvet, the bathroom has Philippe Starck fittings and the 20" LCD screen is accompanied with Bose DVD Surround Sound Theatre. A galley kitchen and a fully stocked minibar are at your disposal, for these holidays are all-inclusive, including the champagne. On deck big cushions provide comfortable support for lounging, sunbathing and gazing out to sea.

The beach bungalows are more prosaic - square and solid without much of beauty to rest your eyes upon. These rooms are more for crashing at the end of a long day than lingering in. The iPod is a great idea, providing immediate access to thousands of tracks to suit your mood - rather than going to reception to sort through a collection of CDs. And the plunge pools in four of the six rooms are large and appealing.

After your return to dry land and before repairing to the bar for cocktail hour you might revel in a spa treatment. I happened to have one of the best massages I've ever had here. Then it's the stroll across the beach again at the end of the day for your evening meal, either on your own somewhere private or communally with your few fellow guests, hosted by David and Jacqueline O'Hara.

Guests quickly come to feel at home here, delving into the bar to get their own cold beer or welcoming new guests as their own. Although this is an ultimate sort of holiday for the rich, it is never precious or pretentious. "It's not about gold taps", says Jacqueline, "it's about feelings and experiences".

Dhoni Mighili is a place where you can make your fantasies happen. For that extra special anniversary event or unforgettable honeymoon it is perfect. Your thakuru is there to make it happen just as you planned it. Finally, and here is the ultimate fantasy, you can take the whole island for yourself and a dozen or so of your closest friends.

1	2	3	4	**5**	6	7	8	9	10		**1**	2	3	4	5	6	7	8	9	10

LOWEST   RELATIVE PRICE   HIGHEST   MOST   ROOM DENSITY   LEAST

T 664 0055 F 664 0066
E info@dhonvelibeach.com
www.dhonvelibeach.com

North Male Atoll

 30 mins

 $4.50

 $3.50

 $4.00

 $51

 $27

Albatross Top Diving

 $62

6 x $372

PADI $487

Dhonveli Beach & Spa

Dhonveli is in the process of going upmarket. It has undergone enormous structural changes, similar to, but to a much lesser extent than, One & Only Reethi Rah.

And in the same way it will take a matter of years before the vegetation grows luxuriantly, the beach is made fine and the lagoon returns to crystal clarity.

It just so happens that this island has one of the best surf breaks in the country and is close by to one or two others. Run since its inception by Tony, an Australian married to a Maldivian, Atoll Adventures looks after an eclectic gathering of surfers, old and young, from around the world. The loose but bonded group hangs out at the corner of the island with the surf point. They have their own bar, their own timetable and rituals and are generally only glimpsed at mealtimes and in the bar. The surfing season is during the southwest monsoon, which is otherwise known as the low season.

The other guests are a mix of Italians, British, French, Russians and Chinese. The Italians might remain a majority but their animation programmes will be soft rather than the full-on club style that it was previously. Nonetheless this is a resort that would suit family fun and activities.

The animation team is the classic profile of bronzed, fit and enthusiastic young men and women whose job it is to tell people what's on, to run the events and to encourage participation. There is one wide and long beach on the island and that is ideal for getting together for aqua gym, fun and games, sunbathing and all the other ways of generally enjoying each other's company.

The bad news is that the beach is far from the Maldivian ideal of sand as soft and fine as icing sugar. This is a man-made beach that is still gritty with coral pieces underfoot. In the water, it must be said, the sand is frequently ideal.

In the middle of the thin island is a large sunset bar, a sizeable peanut-shaped swimming pool with a huge wooden deck and hardcourt badminton and tennis courts. These are fine facilities to grace any five-star but time is needed to bed them into vegetation - from coconut palms to potted flowers - for shade and beauty.

Being close to Male and the international airport and moving upmarket - its next-door neighbour is the Four Seasons - it is thought that a variety of room options is the way to go. There are five land room types and the Waterbungalows offer a few more.

The core of the room design is the same throughout: a thatched roof and light interior with dappled, white plastered walls, a good bathroom, a day bed, tv, hairdryer and safe. The differences are in location, size and details.

The cheapest rooms are the Sunset Villas, which are in two-storey blocks and look out to the sunset but over a rocky or walled shoreline. The other rooms (bar the surfers' Garden Villas) are on the other side of the island around the big beach, facing east or north.

Some Sunrise Cottages face north away from the sun and towards the Waterbungalows. Their floor is of stone effect tiles and they only have a single basin but these are nonetheless fine rooms. Other Sunrise Cottages face east like the Sunrise Villas and top end Vista Suites.

The Sunrise Villas have wooden floors and unusual carved wooden doors and furniture, giving them a somewhat Spanish feel. These are delightfully light and comfortable. The Vista Suites are a tour de force of seven interconnecting circles on two floors. These are large and unquestionably beautiful rooms, with large, whimsical indoor/outdoor bathrooms.

The Waterbungalows are likely to have their own separate reception, restaurant and other facilities, like a premium resort within a resort. The rooms themselves though are somewhat disappointing with the extensive use of hardboard and their narrow lounge, although the deck space is generous.

Diving plays a small part in the resort life at present but there are many excellent sites in the neighbourhood and it will surely become more significant in the future. There is no snorkeling from the island but trips are taken to nearby reefs.

Dhonveli, then, is a resort in transition, hoping one day soon to be placed up there with its illustrious next-door neighbour. Time, hard work and luck might just do it.

| 1 | 2 | 3 | 4 | 5 | 6 | 7 | 8 | 9 | 10 | | 1 | 2 | 3 | 4 | 5 | 6 | 7 | 8 | 9 | 10 |

LOWEST   RELATIVE PRICE   HIGHEST   MOST   ROOM DENSITY   LEAST

T 666 0586   F 666 0514
E info@ellaidhoo.com.mv
www.travelin-maldives.com

North Ari Atoll

 20 mins

 80 mins

 $3.40

 $3.40

 $4

1/2 $37

 $34

Sub Aqua

 $58

6 x $312

PADI $514

Ellaidhoo

This resort recently changed hands again and will be closed for major renovations from the summer of 2007 until the end of the year.

Rooms and restaurants will greatly improve but whatever happens the island's strengths will remain its excellent snorkeling and diving.

The housereef has a consistent drop-off, good corals and wonderful fish life. You can snorkel all the way around the island - or come in at any one of the six cut-throughs. Mantas, sharks and even whale sharks have been seen here. With an intermittent stream of snorkelers heading out near the jetty on the south side (where the best snorkeling is to be found) and other guests idling in the water and sunbathing on the main beach nearby, this is the centre of the day-time action, the place with the buzz.

Just 15 metres from the jetty is a wreck, which at 30 metres down is inaccessible for snorkelers but certainly adds something extra to the fine housereef diving. As the visiting big fish would indicate, there are occasional strong currents here which guests need to be aware of. Drop a handful of sand in the water first or consult the dive school.

The dive school is a remarkably busy and enthusiastic place. Italian divers prefer a morning dive, perhaps a double tank, and then relax in the afternoon. They are serviced by Italian instructors, who also offer a free introductory dive for each of their guests. The German and English divers tend to be more single-minded, many of them on limitless diving packages, with 400 or 500 dives logged. It says a great deal that wherever else they go, they always come back to Ellaidhoo (and it's probably not just for the free tea, chocolate, coconut and water on the boats). The three nearby Protected Marine Areas are just the start of what the region has to offer.

The dive base is at pains to explain, though, that they are not all about experienced diving. They are equally keen to help beginners with the next step. The neighbouring island of Maaga has a fine lagoon for lessons and beginner dives. And sheltered dives are not hard to find, even for full-day trips.

It is a surprise to see such a busy and important place hidden inside the island in a dark, low building with suits and equipment outside. There is talk of a new centre being built on the beach.

The main beach is on the west side (sunset facing), it is wide and wonderful, definitely A grade. Problem is, it's the only beach on the island of any significance. As a general rule, that's OK for Italians but not for others. This oval island with its small lagoon has seen its beaches reduced by the currents of the channel (and the tsunami) to the remnant, though a fine one, on the lee side. This is despite the lagoon walls that encircle the island (actually the first in the country to do so).

A saving grace is the next-door island of Maaga, which belongs to the resort and has been set up as the watersports island, base for diving lessons and general afternoon fun and sun spot. The resort runs a free ferry over every morning and afternoon. And once a week organises the Maaga Beach Party with a barbecue dinner on the beach.

It's a good thing that the watersports are on another island as they can get on with lots of motorised sports without being heard on the resort: fun tubes, jet skis, water skis and knee boards. Other activities and excursions are as expected (fishing, island hopping and Male), though there is only one snorkeling trip a week. If the dive school takes over that will increase to daily.

There is a massive sports centre in the middle of the island. On the second floor are separate rooms for a gleaming, modern gym, for stepping and spinning classes (group cycling) and for two pool tables. Outside are jacuzzis, a tennis court, a squash court and a children's play area. Inside on the ground floor is a big satellite tv, a well-stocked bar, a karaoke lounge and a massage room. Frankly it's all a bit over the top and, well, not much used (it's not cheap).

The rooms are all large with decent bathrooms. There are no real differences between them except their location. The family rooms are in a row behind the others and only a relative few of them face the west beach. There will be new waterbungalows in the west lagoon, which will hopefully not disturb the beach or the view. It would mean reducing an equivalent number of rooms on the island, which would be good, though the overall number would still be high in relation to the island size.

T 664 4776 F 664 2673
E embvil@dhivehinet.net.mv
www.embudu.com

1	**2**	3	4	5	6	7	8	9	10
LOWEST			RELATIVE PRICE			HIGHEST			

1	2	3	4	5	6	7	8	9	10
MOST			ROOM DENSITY				LEAST		

South Male Atoll

 45 mins

 $3.15

$2.10

$3.15

¹/₂ $26

$13

 Diverland

$57

6 x $322

PADI $483

Embudu Village

Working on the principle 'if it ain't broke don't fix it', Embudu Village is a continuing success story.

That success is based on proximity to Male, value for money, a homely atmosphere, a great housereef and top diving.

That's a great formula for success but in Maldives tourism you can't stand still. People's expectations are always rising. Embudu's stock of rooms looks a bit tired now and the landscape a bit 'scuffy', but then the high occupancy makes it difficult to find time to do thoroughgoing renovations.

Somewhat like Maayafushi, the key to this resort is not the built environment but the unhurried, easygoing, feel-at-home atmosphere. This is, of course, aided and abetted by great staff, half of whom have been around for ten years or more, while the redoubtable general manager, Ramsey Pereira, has put in nearly 20 years. You know you're going to get many a "welcome back".

One change has been the building of a new main jetty on the opposite side of the island to the original (for the boats at low tide). Now you don't walk by the ornate bar and through the flowered garden to the reception but skirt alongside the open service area.

The reception/office, coffee shop/lounge and restaurant building, with its metal roof, is dim and hot during the day but comes to life in the evenings when the lighting and conversation work wonders.

The main bar with its wooden platform over the water comes alive at sunset and once a week there's a disco but, essentially, this is a quiet place for recharging the batteries - for the long run back in Europe, and for the short run between snorkeling and diving trips.

Snorkeling is a constant source of pleasure here. Easily accessible through five cut-throughs, the regrowing coral, the many schools of fish (including barracuda) and the big ones such as eagle rays and reef sharks are always on show. And for the truly big ones, the resort puts on manta ray snorkeling trips almost daily when they show up between April and November.

Diving remains popular and enjoyable here. Popular because of the variety of great dives nearby, and enjoyable because the dive base leaders and staff are particularly friendly and accommodating, as well as efficient. The Protected Marine Area of Embudu Channel is a couple of minutes away and encompasses the thrilling drift dive of Embudu Express, the coral gardens of Embudu Thila and a shark point (grey reef sharks).

Nearly three quarters of the guests are German speakers and a quarter are French. The remainder are a few British, Italian and Japanese. Everyone is on full board and all three meals are worth looking forward to - there has been no budget squeeze here. The separate buffet tables and a live cooking station outside have done away with the long queue. The smiling food and beverage manager and his waiters, the excitable chatter among the low lit tables and, most of all, the really good food, make dining one of the day's highlights.

If you've had good food and drink and a busy day diving or snorkeling, then a simple bed might be all you want. Embudu can give you that. Its 36 Standard Rooms are perhaps the only 'old style Maldives' rooms remaining. They do not have a/c, the only hot water is in the shower and - how nostalgic! - there is salt water in the sink taps. The rooms do still have their die-hard fans.

The 72 Superior Rooms add a/c, fresh water, hairdryer and fridge. The furniture is simple but adequate. The 16 Deluxe Rooms are the waterbungalows. Brown rectangular boxes from outside, they are relatively luxurious inside and boast a satellite tv, a safe, a glass panel in the wood floor and a narrow but private balcony.

In line with its 'natural as possible' ideal, there has not been any sand pumping to create artificial beaches and no groynes have been built, although a couple of low walls have been deemed necessary. Bushes are allowed to grow down at the shoreline, which stabilises it but does mean a sometimes intermittent beach. The sand, unadulterated by pumped stuff, is of the highest quality.

Overall, whatever disappointments there might be are forgotten in a short day or two as the great easygoing atmosphere takes you over. This place will long remain a success.

1	2	3	4	5	6	7	8	9	10
LOWEST		RELATIVE PRICE		HIGHEST					

1	2	3	4	5	6	7	8	9	10
MOST			ROOM DENSITY					LEAST	

T 689 8721 F 689 8020
E equator@dhivehinet.net.mv
www.equatorvillage.com

Addu Atoll

 90 mins

 inc

 inc

½  $35

 $15

Diverland

$50

 5 x $276

PADI $535

Equator Village

Equator Village has one big difference from all the other resorts in Maldives. This one is not an island on its own, it is connected to six other islands, inhabited and uninhabited.

This means it is the only resort where you can go off and freely mix with 'real life'. Not for an hour or two on the day you are expected, but at any time. The real pleasure of this resort is cycling off to explore the other islands, to discover for yourself lovely beaches in quiet coconut groves and to casually meet the locals. The level of spoken English here is good, so there is an opportunity not just to look but to interact. The hotel also rents a minibus for half-day trips up the causeway to Hithadu, the country's second largest population after Male.

Germans make up around two thirds of the guests here, with Russians almost all the remainder, and everybody comes on all-inclusive deals. It should be said that the food is basic and the included drinks are far from premium brands. But the atmosphere is usually very good, perhaps because the unique situation of the resort throws people together.

Guests get one Island Hopping and one Night Fishing excursion included in the holiday. They happen just once a week, as does the disco. The other entertainments are a fine full-size snooker table and a good hardcourt tennis court. There are also two free snorkeling trips a day. The housereef itself is just OK.

Diving is the real reason to come here for many of the German guests. By some fluke of channels and currents, Addu Atoll was not affected by the coral bleaching event, so it has kept its outstanding coral gardens. It also boasts year-round mantas and most of the big fish, such as grey reef sharks, tiger sharks, barracudas, yellow fin tunas and napoleon wrasse.

Inside the enclosed atoll the visibility is generally quite poor and the dives are mostly 40 to 50 minutes away, so there are no more than two dives a day plus a weekly night dive. One regular site is the 'British Loyalty', at 140 metres, the biggest wreck in the country.

The other key highlight for many guests is the large, free-form swimming pool with its swim-up bar. A good part of each day is spent on the surrounding sunloungers, reading, chatting and drinking beer or tea. And when the moment takes you, there is a new Indian inspired spa also at the poolside, offering a good mix of massages and body treatments.

The 78 standard rooms are in smart rows behind gardens of clipped grass and tropical flowers. Inside, they are not luxurious but always neat and clean. An internet spot is planned but at my last visit the only means of communication was still the public phone booth near the reception.

The grounds of the hotel, like the whole island of Gan, are wonderfully green, with a variety of indigenous and introduced trees and flowers (and bird life) not found on other islands. Unfortunately, the hotel's beach is not much to write home about, but guests find sufficient room on the sandy path above the narrow beach to relax on loungers and sunbathe.

Over the coming years Addu Atoll will be developing new resorts and Equator Village will surely benefit from this and improve. At the moment, one gets the feeling of being on the adventurous edge of Maldives tourism. Holidays are very well priced here but they are also unique for the opportunity to see real Maldives life.

| 1 | 2 | 3 | **4** | 5 | 6 | 7 | 8 | 9 | 10 |
LOWEST   RELATIVE PRICE   HIGHEST

| 1 | **2** | 3 | 4 | 5 | 6 | 7 | 8 | 9 | 10 |
MOST   ROOM DENSITY   LEAST

T 664 4487 F 664 5926
E eriyadu@aaa.com.mv
www.aaa-resortsmaldives.com

North Male Atoll

 50 mins

 $3.85

 $3.30

 $4.40

 $40

 $17

Werner Lau

 $68

6 x $388

PADI $560

Eriyadu

Small, quiet and laid back, with good snorkeling, good diving and good food all at a reasonable price. That is Eriyadu in a nutshell.

The island enjoys an ideal position alone and just behind the outside rim of its atoll. This means that divers rarely need to travel far and rarely need to share their dive sites. It also, usually, means the island has a close by reef and a good beach.

The beach has diminished over the years, like so many other resorts, but the quality remains superb. The very fine sand moves around the island with the seasons. The last numbered rooms, on the west side, are the ones to go for during the low season - sunset and a broad fine beach is hard to beat. During the high season the beach moves away from here and is more evenly spread around the northern side where most of the rooms are.

Wherever the room is it will be just a short swim away from the housereef drop-off. And it is possible to snorkel all the way around the island. With a tank service to the three exit points, this is also a big bonus for divers.

Diving naturally plays a big part in the resort's life. The centre is on its own jetty alongside its boats, which makes things easy and convenient. As with all of this group's resorts the base is run by the renowned Werner Lau. His website comprehensively covers all the sites and sights they offer, as well as prices and procedures.

All but two of the 60 Superior Rooms are in pairs and there is a block with six standard rooms. On such a small island this is a bit of a squeeze. Having said that, there is a good growth of trees and bushes separating the rooms for privacy. The cover also affords good shade between the rooms and the beach (although there are sadly few picturesque coconut palms).

Inside, the rooms are cool, dim and comfortable. The parquet flooring is dark hardwood and the wardrobes and tables are also dark brown with brass fittings. In addition to a safe, hairdryer and well-stocked minibar there is a satellite tv and a four-channel radio. The bathrooms have recently been redone to a decent standard.

In the same building as the reception is a good gym room and an area with a pool table, table tennis table, table football and dartboard. In the thatched bar over the water there's a disco once a week and a live band every other week. It also serves drinks until the last person leaves but that is rarely very late as this is essentially a slow, quiet place.

The atmosphere of the place is laid back. There is no need to wear sandals anywhere at any time, even though the reception and restaurant have shiny tiled floors and the bar has wooden floorboards. Guests are generally left to their own devices as the management is rather withdrawn.

Half the guests here are German and the other half are made up of Swiss, British, Italian, French, Japanese and Russian. Around half are on full board and half on half board. Whichever basis you choose you won't be disappointed. The food here (as with all the resorts in this group) is far better than you could reasonably expect.

All the meals are buffet, varying every night and including Maldivian, Mediterranean, Chinese and a barbecue on the beach. Repeaters, of whom there are many, get a special seafood dinner on the beach. Desserts too are very good.

All in all, this is a small, straightforward island with some key selling points: price, food, snorkeling, diving and a peaceful atmosphere.

1	2	3	**4**	5	6	7	8	9	10
LOWEST		RELATIVE PRICE		HIGHEST					

1	**2**	3	4	5	6	7	8	9	10
MOST			ROOM DENSITY			LEAST			

T 664 2903 F 664 3803
E fiha@dhivehinet.net.mv
www.fihalhohi.net

South Male Atoll

 75 mins

 $3.85

 $3.85

 $3.85

 $35

 $12

 Ocean Venture

 $59

6 x $336

PADI $510

Fihalhohi

In a quiet corner of South Male Atoll Fihalhohi continues to offer its good honest product to a contented clientele.

With longstanding partnerships with a few major tour operators and little fuss or promotion, this resort remains a hit with the families and couples who have discovered it and recommend it.

An island so rich in mature palms and native trees is rare among the resorts. It is a visual feast as well as practical, for the shade between the rooms and the beach is ideal for children to play in and for adults to lounge in (on deck-chairs or in hammocks) during the heat of the day.

The sand is like icing sugar still, as pumping has not been resorted to, but the extent of the beaches has diminished over the years and a couple of sections of wall have even been built to hold back the erosion. Still there is enough good beach to go around, only a little walking might be necessary if you want a wide beach.

The room standards have gone up as they are nearly all newly built or refurbished and all include a safe, hairdryer and fridge. There is a telephone as well but only for internal calls. The Waterbungalows have tea and coffee sachets and a CD player.

The 114 Comfort Rooms differ from the 24 Classic Rooms only in having a little bit more space, a bathtub with the shower, and a/c included (you must pay extra for the Classic a/c controller). They are also in blocks of four, two up and two down. Designed to put you at your ease, the style is unpretentious and homely, which is typical of the whole resort.

The 12 Waterbungalows are the newest rooms and clearly of a higher standard. Guests enjoy a four-poster bed and comfy chairs and settee, finer quality furniture, more space and a good bathroom with a separate shower. The verandahs of the beach rooms are tiled and a bit small, whereas the deck of the Waterbungalows are large, wooden and in three parts - one outside the bedroom, one outside the bathroom and one platform close to the water. From here you can slip into the water for good swimming and snorkeling.

The extra rooms that have been built have put a bit of a squeeze on the best beach space and on the restaurant space. Most tables are now tables for four and mealtimes are busy with people passing through and noisy with cheerful hubbub and chairs scraping on the tiled floor. The variety of buffets is excellent, with a different nationality or style for every night of the week for two weeks. If it is not of the highest standard, there is always an alternative at the Surf Café, a small, quiet restaurant and coffee shop on the other side of the island.

The Surf Café is connected to the Blue Lagoon Bar and sits by the watersports centre and just behind a fine beach facing west. Guests naturally flock here around sunset. The bar stays open until the last guest goes to bed but it remains a quiet spot, with no music being played, as a deliberate alternative to the main Fisherman's Bar, which has something going on every night.

The two-week programme in the Fisherman's Bar includes all the usual favourites from crab race to karaoke, disco and live music. Some evenings can go long into the night but generally people head off to bed fairly early. The reasons for this are the number of families who come to Fihalhohi, the general air of quiet and relaxation, and the number of guests who tire themselves out with snorkeling and diving.

The housereef is nearby for two thirds of the way around the island and the coral and fish life is decent. The nearby dive spots are also decent but the sites on the other side of the atoll (still very accessible by dhoni) are some of the best known in the country, around Guraidhu, Kandooma and Cocoa. Manta rays and whale sharks are frequent in that area from September through to December.

Enjoying this comfortable, value-for-money family holiday are a majority of Germans and Swiss with the remaining third being British, French and Italian.

T 674 0025 F 674 0024
E fili@aaa.com.mv
www.aaa-resortsmaldives.com

1	2	3	4	5	6	7	8	9	10
LOWEST   RELATIVE PRICE   HIGHEST

1	2	3	4	5	6	7	8	9	10
MOST   ROOM DENSITY   LEAST

Faafu Atoll

 35 mins

 $5

 $3.50

 $2.50

1/2 $25

 $15

Werner Lau

 $76

6 x $445

PADI $500

Filitheyo

Filitheyo scores high marks in all the categories that define a good resort. The fact that it isn't among the most expensive in the country makes it possibly the best in its class.

Let's start with the beach. Not a single groyne breaks the view or the walk down either side of the island. The beach is broad down the side with the large lagoon and narrower on the other side, where the reef is close to shore. Only a very few rooms are occasionally without a stretch of sand, but the reward for not filling in with pumped sand is the feel of talcum powder softness beneath your feet wherever you go.

If you want to go barefoot for your entire holiday you can, as a wooden walkway through the public area is the only change from the sandy floors and the trails that criss-cross the interior. And as for the interior, it's another plus point because few resorts beat this one for impressive stands of mature coconut palms, indigenous vegetation and the chance to walk through and not just around the island.

Most of the rooms are Superiors and face east to the narrower beach. The upside is the ease of access to the reef edge snorkeling. The Deluxe rooms face sunset and have the better beach, though the lagoon is shallow at low tide and can be a bit 'corally'. Both room types share the same low-lit casual comfort and the same cotton and light wood furnishing. The Deluxe rooms are individual as opposed to 'semi-detached', are a little bit bigger and have lovely, extended inside/outside bathrooms.

The Water Villas have similar furniture in a still larger setting, while here the day or third bed of the land rooms becomes a sofa. The deck has a fine Maldivian swing joli, two cushioned sunloungers and steps down to excellent snorkeling. All very lovely, except that you are open to your neighbours on both sides. With three very different aspects to the three room types, a number of guests are splitting their holiday into two or even all three rooms categories and the staff are happy to manage this.

With a channel on both sides of the island, the housereef is a popular dive by day and night. Staff from the dive school will deliver the equipment to benches adjacent to the eight reef cut-throughs. Coral regrowth has been very good and fish life is abundant here and in the whole neighbourhood (as I write it is still the only resort in the atoll, though a couple more are planned). There are shallow thilas inside the atoll for inexperienced divers and many channel dives very close by (with some challenging channel crossings) where the big fish are often encountered. The Werner Lau website is impressively detailed in both German and English.

The resort has moved from being a largely German-speaking dive-oriented island to one with a more cosmopolitan profile. German speakers make up around 40% of guests, British 25%, French 20% and then a mix of other Europeans and Japanese. And although the resort doesn't go out of its way to encourage children and families, it treats them very well and is consequently very popular with them. All this has boosted the liveliness of the place whilst it still retains a calm atmosphere overall.

The delightful 'rustic' bar has a two-hour 'happy hour', a wide selection of cocktails and ice coffees and is flanked by open-sided, thatched games rooms and outdoor tables that run down to the water's edge. It also lists a great little snack menu, from nachos to more substantial meals.

Dining, in fact, is another of the key pleasures of Filitheyo. In my opinion the cuisine is definitely the best in this category of resorts. There is a commitment to quality and presentation that is not often matched and a clear love of the task and invention that is even rarer. With great meal options in the main bar, the à la carte sunset restaurant, villa dining, beach dining and even desert island dining, half board is a good choice to make, especially as guests can choose lunch or dinner as the included meal.

I can see Filitheyo gaining a stronger and stronger reputation as the years go by. I think it's great.

| 1 | 2 | 3 | 4 | 5 | 6 | 7 | 8 | 9 | 10 |

LOWEST   RELATIVE PRICE   HIGHEST

| 1 | 2 | 3 | 4 | 5 | 6 | 7 | 8 | 9 | 10 |

MOST   ROOM DENSITY   LEAST

T 664 2010   F 664 1979
E sales@unient.com.mv
www.universalresorts.com

North Male Atoll

20 mins

45 mins

$4.95

$3.85

$4.40

1/2 $27

$25

Eurodivers

$67

5 x $302

PADI $519

Full Moon

One of the first resorts in the country, this island has gone through several incarnations.

The latest major renovation moves Full Moon solidly upmarket and prioritises its accommodation, beaches, swimming pool and spa experience. Re-establishing the shade and vegetation will take some time.

This is an up and down kind of island, with the main jetty at the tip, all the waterbungalows down one side and the beach rooms down the other, with the service area taking over the bottom part. The beach rooms are on the south side and the beach here is excellent. For strolling through talcum powder sand or sunbathing at any time of day, this beach is one of the resort's main assets.

Towards the narrow, jetty tip of the island there is more beach on both sides, with thatched umbrellas and sunloungers, but this is pumped and not so perfect. It is good sunbathing space for the four Water Villas and one Water Suite, but as the other 52 Waterbungalows parade down the north side there is less and less access to beach.

Two of the Water Villas and a few of the Water-bungalows (where the island bulges) face west to the sunset from their decks. The others face north, though the sun hits their decks for part of the day. The reef drop-off is reachable from the Water Villas and Water Suite but not from the Waterbungalows, though the swimming is good everywhere. The interior design and facilities are first class.

Of the two categories of beach rooms, the 44 Beach Deluxe Rooms are the more economic. They stand in blocks of four, two up and two down, between the Beach Cottage Rooms and the Waterbungalows with their own little beach on the north side. These Deluxe Rooms don't have the tv or cd player that the other rooms have nor the interior decor details but they are very satisfactory. The furniture is of good quality wood and the bathroom is attractively tiled, though the verandah could be larger.

The Beach Cottage Rooms are really splendid rooms. Large, comfortable and very stylish. From the rustic thatched roof to the half open-air bathroom and out to the hibiscus lined verandah, everything speaks of old style comfort within a modern look. The a/c is concealed and silent, the teak furniture is attractive and the satellite tv is best viewed from the bed.

The 55 Beach Cottage Rooms are arranged in four horseshoe shapes, or closes, one next to the other. This does mean that only the end rooms are next to the beach and water, though it's only a matter of some strides across the garden in front to the water's edge. I say garden but the ground is a bit coarse still and it will take some time for the flowers and trees to fulfil their potential.

The central path from the rooms up to the public area and beyond is open to the midday blaze. The public area, on the other hand, is still surrounded by lush growth and attractive flowers. Then again, there is also a great deal of hard flooring of one type or another here, some wood decking but mostly tiles of various sizes and styles.

The swimming pool plays a prominent role in the resort day. Set between the main bar, the lobby and the restaurants, it is large, free form and ideal for that long lazy day sunbathing, chatting and being served drinks and snacks under the parasol.

Unusually three quarters of the guests here are on bed and breakfast deals. Perhaps for this reason the breakfast spread in the main restaurant is very good, with a variety of quality breads and pastries, savoury dishes, fruits and even a Sri Lankan breakfast. All the lunches and five of the seven dinners in the restaurant are then set plates, while guests on bed and breakfast try out the other outlets, which are a coffee shop, a Barbecue Grill, a Thai and a Mediterranean restaurant.

The Sen Spa, on its own little island connected with a walkway, is a new addition to Full Moon. It is extensive, handsome and well staffed. Again it will take a little while to beautify the setting and develop a bit of its own magic.

The dive school is run by the established Eurodivers and offers a full service (including rinsing and hanging up after dives). There is not much snorkeling to speak of inside the lagoon and though the drop-off is accessible it is not recommended, as the current could be strong in the channels. The hotel puts on a daily, charged, snorkel trip to compensate.

Two thirds of the guests are British and many have been coming year after year. Undisturbed by the reconstruction, they comment on the relationship built up with the staff, of the welcome, remembered preferences and the little extras. The other third of guests are mostly from Japan and the new markets of Russia and China.

1	2	3	4	5	6	7	**8**	9	10			1	2	3	4	5	**6**	7	8	9	10
LOWEST		RELATIVE PRICE					HIGHEST					MOST			ROOM DENSITY					LEAST	

T 666 0505   F 666 0506
E gangehi@clubvacanze.com.mv
www.clubvacanze.it

North Ari Atoll

20 mins

120 mins

300 mins

inc

inc

inc

inc

inc

Club Vacanze

inc

5 x   inc

PADI $400

Gangehi

Small, beautiful and very high class. Those are the basics; the real story is that there is some magic to this place.

Good things happen on Gangehi. And much of the reason for that is owing to Monica.

Monica has been in Maldives since the very beginning of tourism and has been connected with Gangehi for most of that time. "It's like my house now", she says, and she makes the whole resort like a house for her guests. She sets the calm, adult atmosphere that pervades the place. Her continuing presence and fluent Dhivehi (the language of Maldives) has forged a loyalty among the staff that is rare, and a part of the magic.

The resort used to have a beach problem, with no sand for the beach bungalows and the water-bungalows stranded on a beach, but this has been completely overcome by pumping. Pumped sand is not as fine as original beach sand and some walls have been built in the lagoon, but now there is beach all around and the waterbungalows are over the water.

A permanent feature is the lovely sandbank that stretches into the lagoon from beside the bar and lounge and restaurant. Soft, white and very fine, the open stretch is ideal for the more communal times - from sunbathing to bocce. And it is from here that guests walk out to the reef edge to snorkel or dive.

Just 25 rooms make this the second smallest resort in the country (after Kudahithi). There is, nonetheless, considerable variety in the room locations. Two Beach Bungalows are tucked behind a little vegetation at the very start of the sandbank. Three more are hidden in the jungle interior and the other 12 are strung around the perimeter from south to northeast, with good privacy but varying amounts of sun, beach and vegetation. The eight Waterbungalows are individual but paired on a jetty and all face west from their large, private deck.

The Waterbungalows are larger than the Beach Bungalows but otherwise very similar. The interiors are spacious, cool and dim. Dark wood is used extensively, combined with covers and curtains that pick up the black, brown and white designs of the great Maldivian Thundu Kunaa mats. Tinted glass sliding doors show off the great views but keep the interior shaded and private.

90% of guests here are from Italy but, though it is run entirely by Club Vacanze, it is too smart a place to be run in a club style and any non-Italian that liked the sound of the place is welcome and would surely rejoice at their choice.

It is not a club, then, but there is somehow a sense of being bound together. Everyone comes on an all-inclusive basis. There is just one restaurant, one bar and lounge and a small routine of events and entertainments that mould the day and the week.

There is no need to sign for anything, as everything is included. Even diving is included. With few guests and fewer divers, attention is on an individual basis and the diving is terrific. Gangehi is located in a quiet corner of North Ari Atoll with no competition for nearby sites and within striking distance of some world famous sites to the south as well as the hammerhead shark spot of Rasdhoo to the east.

Finally, the dining is second to none. Five and six star resorts are coming up around the country and the food standard continues to soar but still dinner on Gangehi is not surpassed. Breakfast and lunch are large buffets but dinner is served at the table. That is to say, eight to ten courses on a weekday, 12 on the weekend and up to 17 courses for Easter and Christmas days. Never heavy, never too much, varied and perfectly paced. What a delight that is.

Gangehi is a delight all round. You'll want to string the experience out as far as possible, and then come back the following year.

| 1 | 2 | 3 | 4 | **5** | 6 | 7 | 8 | 9 | 10 | | 1 | 2 | **3** | 4 | 5 | 6 | 7 | 8 | 9 | 10 |

LOWEST   RELATIVE PRICE   HIGHEST   MOST   ROOM DENSITY   LEAST

T 672 0014 F 672 0013
E hakura@dhivehinet.net.mv
www.johnkeellshotels.com

Meemu Atoll

 40 mins

 inc

inc

$4.40

1/2 $30

$30

Dive & Sail

$47

8 x $360

PADI $460

Hakuraa Club

In some key ways Hakuraa Club is much better now than it used to be; it offers a genuinely good value-for-money holiday. The large, very shallow lagoon, however, remains a drawback.

Having reconstructed all the waterbungalows, guests, when they enter for the first time, now let out an involuntary "oh yes" or draw a sharp intake of breath. The size and style is impressive. The all-wood floor and solid wooden furniture give warmth to the simple modernity of the design. Light floods in from the back wall and the glass panels in the sides and floor. The furnishing is classy, the a/c quiet and efficient and the satellite tv and tea and coffee-making facility are appreciated. An ante-room at the entrance is useful for the luggage and wardrobe. The bathroom is smallish but smart and the shower is strong (though you stand in the tub).

The view from the verandah is empty and serene, and side fences afford a fair amount of privacy. Steps lead down to the water but only towards high tide are you able to swim away. At other times you can laze around or wade into the distance.

Owing to the size of the lagoon there is no direct access to the reef for snorkeling but the resort puts on two boats a day to take guests, free of charge, from the end of the jetty to the reef inside the atoll. The snorkeling is not spectacular so you may use your free snorkel and mask to go on one of the twice-weekly snorkeling safaris.

The diving in the region is fresh and unaffected as this is one of only two resorts and nine small inhabited islands in the whole atoll. There is one big channel not too far away that provides several fine sites for both novices and experts and an inter-atoll cargo shipwreck for variety, though thilas and giris are the mainstay.

The dive school is at the end of the 500-metre jetty, so regular divers should ask for a nearer one of the 70 waterbungalows or perhaps go for one of the ten beach rooms. The beach rooms are a little less impressive than the waterbungalows but they are private and located just behind the beach.

The beach itself is not of the finest sand but it is broad, open to the sun all day and runs right down one side of the curved island. The waterbungalows run down the whole of the other side.

No watersports are included in the package but the big, shallow lagoon is just what beginners need, although the bottom has a lot of coral pieces.

The all-inclusive package covers non-premium brand drinks, wine at meals, soft drinks and tea and coffee. The three themed buffets a day are rightly very well received and so is the daily high tea at four. High tea is taken in the new main bar built over the water at the start of the jetty. It's a fine place that really comes to life in the evenings with drinking, chatter, games and organised entertainments.

Adding greatly to the changes at Hakuraa Club is the top management that has done a great job in making it a fun and friendly place, whilst also being efficient and helpful. Although the geography of the island is not perfect there are precious few complaints from the guests, as overall they recognise that the food, the rooms, the diving, the sunbathing and the atmosphere are all well worth the price.

1 2 3 **4** 5 6 7 8 9 10
LOWEST RELATIVE PRICE HIGHEST

1 2 3 **4** 5 6 7 8 9 10
MOST ROOM DENSITY LEAST

T 664 4615 F 664 2881
E manager@helengeli.net
www.helengeli.net

North Male Atoll

 15 mins

 120 mins

 $3.50

 $2.50

$5

$39

Ocean Pro

$66

5 x $330

PADI $619

Helengeli

Helengeli has long been among the very best dive islands in the country. After a change of owners and an upgrade, it is now very much more than that.

Comfortable, handsome and conspicuously well managed, it is great for anyone looking for a peaceful holiday, including singles and couples with children. My top tip: if partying and beaches aren't your priorities, this is unmatched value for money.

A resort with 60% or more divers is never going to be a late night drinking and dancing place. Indeed, there is no organised evening entertainment at all here. Having said that, it isn't by any means dead in the evenings and some nights do take off.

But essentially this is an ultra quiet island. With so many out during the day diving or on an excursion (and no thought of animation) this is a place to potter around, swim, snorkel, kick back and truly relax. A Duniya Spa is there to help the process along.

The rocky end of the island that faces the open ocean is closed to guests, and currents in the channels on both sides work against long, broad beaches. However, a good half of the 50 rooms have some beach (the first numbered) and a permanent sand bar at the other end is never more than a short stroll away. Never augmented with pumped sand, the beaches, in terms of quality, are as good as they get. Furthermore, with no groynes or walls and a proper concern for the natural environment, the setting is always pleasing to the eye.

The rooms themselves are nothing special, old-fashioned and basic, but they do have a hairdryer, safe and reasonably priced minibar (no phone or tv). They contrast with the new public area, which is delightful and really gives the resort an attractive central focus.

As befits a small resort, the reception is little more than a desk on the sand, with a thatched roof above. The fair-sized swimming pool between it and the bar is good for laps or playing and is surrounded by a wide deck that looks out to sea. The bar is open on all sides, has deep-cushioned low seating on the sandy floor and is an all round pleasant place to meet, drink and chat.

Flowing on from there is the restaurant. Built in the same style, it has open sides, sand on the floor and a light colour scheme. Lunch is always buffet and dinner is a mix of set plate and buffets, with a regular live pasta station. The fare is not haute cuisine but varied and well cooked. Vegetarians are looked after well and the kitchen is overseen by the head chef of the great Mirihi, which has to be good news.

The whole of the public area is covered by an internet hotspot, which is a surprise on a dedicated dive island. As well as a good children's pool, baby-sitting is available at any time and the attitude of the staff to children is excellent.

As to the diving, I hardly need to talk about it as the dedicated clientele are fully briefed on the options from past experience and from the Ocean Pro website. This is a resort where the divers know their stuff. Learners are willingly accommodated but most of the divers are experienced to very experienced.

All alone in the northeast corner of North Male Atoll, Helengeli has the luxury of a whole raft of fine dive sites almost to itself. As the saying goes, there are no bubble dives. Fish life in the region is extremely rich, from myriad schools of small reef fish to turtles, sharks, barracuda and tuna and, in season, mantas and whale sharks. One of the finest thilas anywhere is just six minutes from the island, called, unsurprisingly, Helengeli Thila.

The housereef itself is excellent for diving and six entry points and a tank service from the dive centre make this a very popular option. Black tip reef sharks, rays, groupers and octopuses are a few of the highlights during the day. At night, the lobster cave comes alive. The housereef is close to shore all around the island, so snorkeling is easy and very rewarding.

The new, improved Helengeli is a gem.

| 1 | 2 | 3 | 4 | 5 | 6 | 7 | 8 | **9** | 10 | | 1 | 2 | 3 | 4 | 5 | **6** | 7 | 8 | 9 | 10 |

LOWEST　　RELATIVE PRICE　　HIGHEST　　　MOST　　ROOM DENSITY　　LEAST

T 668 0629 F 668 0619
E maldives@hilton.com
www.hiltonworldresorts.com

All images courtesy of Hilton

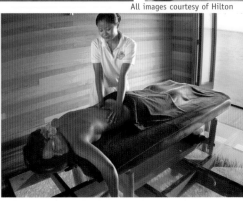

South Ari Atoll

 35 mins

$6

$4.50

$6.50

$83

$39

Sub Aqua

$90

5 x $415

PADI $710

Hilton

The remade Hilton Maldives has gone beyond what you expect of Hilton to a position amongst the very finest resorts in the country.

The chic magazines that thought they knew Hilton are now beating a path to its jetty to find out what's happened.

What has happened is the creation of three fantasy destinations over two islands by one impressive Hilton Resort and Spa team - three Maldives dreams designed and delivered to the very best of human capabilities.

The spa is not a new idea fitted into the existing set-up, as it is on most other resorts, but a separate dream destination in itself. The Spa Village sits entirely on stilts over the water and is only connected by wooden walkway to the outside world.

Each lovely, light and spacious bungalow has its own treatment room (wonderfully lit with blue spots) and an open balcony that entices you to plunge into the water below. With its own restaurant serving healthy but tasty cuisine, a gym and the main spa itself, guests can experience the spa atmosphere every minute of their holiday.

On offer are four, seven and ten-day packages on generous full board basis with daily lifestyle and wellness consultations and one treatment per day. For those who are not ultra spa purists the packages can be combined with a longer stay in one or even both of the other Hilton Maldives environments.

Just across the walkway is the island of the beach villas, Rangalifinolhu. It is larger than the island of the water villas, Rangali, but that is just the beginning of the differences. The fantasy-made-real here is about new heights and new experiences in leisure, in a fun atmosphere of friendliness and activity.

Having flattened every building on the island Hilton have constructed a theatre of holiday pleasures. The 44 Deluxe Beach Villas are the largest such rooms in the country (at 300 square metres). The 35 Beach Villas, with no garden or pool, are half the size but equal in luxury and spectacular interior design, with sliding glass walls to the beach in front and a fountain courtyard behind. Even the content of the minibar is new and exciting!

The Atoll Market Place is real culinary theatre where the restaurant is the kitchen and the kitchen is the restaurant. The eight distinct show kitchens inspire you with their own sights, sounds and smells then delight you with their tastes. Yet even more theatrical than this is the now justly famous glass underwater restaurant. I was ready to be disappointed but was knocked out by its success and originality.

If that wasn't enough, there are tastings and dinners in the expansive wine cellar hosted by the chef, the sommelier and the country's only cheese specialist. This is all done in an unpretentious manner, in keeping with the atmosphere of the island as a whole and the bar, lounge and (large, infinity) pool area in particular. At this point I might mention the best lighting by far anywhere in Maldives.

Across the 500-metre bridge on Rangali Island the priorities are very different. Here it is all about one's own space and privacy, about receiving and expecting the very finest goods and services, about a sense of being élite. It is also about peace, quiet and romance.

The five categories of Water Villas run from gorgeous to outrageous. Increasingly large and well appointed, they are all luxurious, from their wide wooden decks facing west to the Bulgari amenities in the 'plain' Water Villas and the Philippe Starck fittings and revolving bed in the Sunset Water Villas.

The island has its own over-water spa using even more exclusive products, a restaurant of even higher standards and views out to the open ocean (next stop East Africa) that are even finer than those on Rangalifinolhu.

The built environment and the service provided are both so faultless that it rarely comes to mind that the resort isn't, in fact, perfect. The lagoon is occasionally shallow enough to restrict swimming - particularly between the two islands, the beach is extensive but not of the finest sand, and there is no quality housereef snorkeling to speak of. These are not insignificant considerations by any means but, on the other hand, until perfection is achieved elsewhere the Hilton Maldives will do very nicely indeed.

T 668 0011 F 668 0022
E info@holiday-island.com.mv

1	2	3	4	**5**	6	7	8	9	10
LOWEST		RELATIVE PRICE		HIGHEST					

1	2	3	**4**	5	6	7	8	9	10
MOST			ROOM DENSITY				LEAST		

South Ari Atoll

 35 mins

150 mins

 $4.40

$3.30

$4.95

$55

$35

Villa Diving

$52

5 x $250

PADI $369

Holiday Island

Holiday Island changed from being a popular resort with a mixed clientele to an exclusively Italian (Club Venta) resort. It is now going back to the international mix.

Former returnees and new devotees could revive it to the times when it won the highest occupancy award (1997), but it needs to redefine its place in an ever more demanding market.

For Italians, there is no 'all-together beach', which is a key requirement - that is, somewhere to hang out together during the day and enjoy the organised fun and games. The evening cabaret is also no longer functioning. None of this is a problem for other nationalities. The days are quiet and peaceful and the nights are social. Karaoke takes place twice a week, a live band and cultural show once a week each. Otherwise it's chatting and drinking in the bar and table tennis and snooker in the lobby.

Villa resorts promote the image of having lots on offer all day long, but Holiday Island would seem to be now more about the original Maldives style of an unchanged island where you go to relax and soak up the sun. If the urge for action and a change of atmosphere comes on, there are frequent ferries over to the neighbouring island, which happens to be the biggest and brashest resort in the country, another Villa resort called Sun Island. There you can avail yourself of the fine sports facilities, the large swimming pool, the spa, the restaurants and even the video games room before sailing back to the quiet haven of Holiday.

As a result of former training by the Italian chefs, the food here is well above average. There is variety and quality in the buffets and live cooking stations for the meat, pasta dishes and occasionally even the dessert (pears flambé). The restaurant itself is large and airy, with no requirement to double up on tables.

The 142 rooms are all individual bungalows, except for the nine interconnecting family rooms. Solid, bright and clean, they have all the usual ingredients, plus a satellite television, hairdryer and bidet. Not all the rooms are the same, though, when it comes to location.

Half the rooms face north and half face south - and it's always preferable to face south. Furthermore, the rooms on the northeast corner (101-135) face a beach with a bad erosion problem (a vertical drop of a metre and more). The sand quality for most of the island is OK but is excellent at the western end. So the rooms to get are those on the southwest where the beach line takes a turn, increasing the sense of privacy, where the sand is superb and the sun shines all day and sets within view (rooms 170-185).

It surprised me to see so many wooden sunloungers on the beach without the cushioned covers, but not when I discovered guests have to pay a dollar a day to rent them. Not good. The 300 metre trip to the housereef from the jetty is also charged for. That's $5 per trip and $5 a day for the snorkeling equipment.

Most people are on all-inclusive packages, but it's not straightforward. The perfectly positioned beach bar is only open for three two-hour slots a day and beer is the only alcohol served gratis for AI clients. Then, sitting on the wooden deck shared by the bar and the coffee shop, you need to pay for a drink if it is ordered from a coffee shop waiter but it's free if ordered from a bar waiter. The opportunities for misunderstandings are many. On the other hand, the Maldivian supervisors are excellent at smoothing over any little problems. And the waiters are also excellent at their job, smiling and serving with a good line in conversation.

This region of southeast Ari Atoll is world famous for its diving. The channels attract the big fish, the sharks and pelagics; the thilas have large schools of the little fish and the outside sites are home to roving whale sharks. This should be a good reason to base yourself here. This, the peace and quiet and the occasional trips to Sun.

| 1 | 2 | 3 | 4 | 5 | 6 | 7 | 8 | 9 | 10 |
LOWEST   RELATIVE PRICE   HIGHEST

| 1 | 2 | 3 | 4 | 5 | 6 | 7 | 8 | 9 | 10 |
MOST   ROOM DENSITY   LEAST

T 664 4222 F 664 4333
E info@huvafenfushi.com
www.huvafenfushi.com

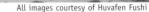

All images courtesy of Huvafen Fushi

North Male Atoll

 15 mins

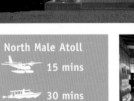 30 mins

$6

$6.50

$9

1 $100

$35

Divers Haven

$84

6 x $488

PADI $700

Huvafen Fushi

Huvafen Fushi is the sister island to Dhoni Mighili and they share the concept of taking a dream and making it real.

The dream that Dhoni Mighili fulfils is the one where you live on a luxury boat being served by a personal butler as you drift between idyllic equatorial islands. Huvafen Fushi delivers the dream that has you and your partner living like the jet set, surrounded by the finest luxuries modern life has to offer, indulging in haute cuisine and 'haute spa'. It is life taken from the pages of Condé Nast Traveller, Harper's Bazaar and World of Interiors.

There are three categories of land rooms and water-bungalows. They share the same luxury elements - the plunge pool, the plasma tv and Bose surround sound, the Frette linen and L'Occitane amenities - and the same commitment to high design. What differentiates them is a greater level of design, plus size and location. Plunge pools become large plunge pools then pools, 32" plasma televisions grow to 60" and floorspace expands from 125 sqm to 160 sqm to 800 sqm for the land rooms and 130 sqm to 160 sqm to 330 sqm for the waterbungalows.

All eight Beach Bungalows and two Deluxe Beach Bungalows face more or less north, while the other six Deluxe Beach Bungalows face south to all-day sunshine. The beach bungalow side has the wider and longer beach (you can walk along uninterrupted) and slopes gently into the empty, sandy lagoon whereas the deluxe bungalow side is close to the reef for snorkeling. The beaches outside the deluxe rooms themselves, it should be said, are very good.

The top rooms in each category secure their privacy at the extreme ends of the resort. The single Beach Pavilion commands a swathe of south-facing beach (with a low retaining wall) and is built for pure indulgence. The master bedroom on the upper storey looks out through floor-to-ceiling glass widows and down through a glass floor to the inside/outside infinity pool. The two Ocean Pavilions are a hundred metres further along the waterbungalow jetty and face directly to the sunset from the deck surrounding the infinity pool that flows from inside the room.

The difference between the other waterbungalows, beyond the expanded sizes and design details, is in their names. The 12 Lagoon Bungalows look from north to east into the lagoon, the 12 Ocean Bungalows look from south to west for sunshine or sunset on the deck as well as easy access to snorkeling the reef.

With just 43 rooms there are three very different restaurants and five private dining venues, not including the rooms. There is the shallow end of the underlit infinity pool, the sandbank, wine cellar, yoga pavilion, underwater spa and a candlelit groyne above the water.

Most people come on a bed and breakfast basis and then choose between the main restaurant ('Celsius') for buffets and à la carte, the fine seafood dining restaurant ('Salt') for Mediterranean fused with Southeast Asian, and the healthy dining restaurant ('Raw') for beautiful minimalist food and juices inspired by and coordinated with the spa. The island sommelier also hosts a five-course meal matched with a few of the 700 labels in the impressive wine cellar ('Vinum').

The intention is to develop the cuisine and spa reputation to the point where guests come for that combination alone. Huvafen Fushi is still relatively young and I would put Cocoa and Taj Exotica ahead of it at the top of the shortlist at the moment.

What nobody else has is an underwater spa. The anticipation as you descend is fulfilled by the thrill of seeing emerge from the blue light iridescent pink and green parrotfish, batfish and hundreds of wrasses and anemone fish, all magnified by the thick glass. Then you lie face down on a table - where a mirror placed below you allows you to continue the experience.

The treatments and the therapists are mostly from Bali and Thailand, concentrating on well-being, beauty and rejuvenation. For deeper states an Indian Yogi is there to take morning and late afternoon sessions in the separate pavilion over the water. And a mention should be made of the relaxation room on top of the spa, which is wide open to the sunset and sunrise sides and has a particularly good feel.

Huvafen Fushi is a beautiful place to look at and wonderfully indulgent to live in. It is perfectly situated within its own lagoon, not far from the airport and with good snorkeling and a fine beach. The one thing that just seems to be missing at the moment is the collective heartbeat. That united love of a place that all the staff draw from and contribute to. But that could well come with time. **91**

T 650 1515 F 650 1616
E sales@island-hideaway.com
www.island-hideaway.com

1	2	3	4	5	6	7	8	9	10
LOWEST   RELATIVE PRICE   HIGHEST

1	2	3	4	5	6	7	8	9	10
MOST   ROOM DENSITY   LEAST

Images above courtesy of Island Hideaway

Haa Alifu Atoll

 45 mins

 +

 20 mins

 $6.60

 $4.40

$4.40

1/2 $55

$90

Meridis

$92

PADI $698

Island Hideaway

Island Hideaway is an apt name for this resort, which is not only in a quiet corner of a distant northern atoll, it is also a large island with just 43 rooms concealed amidst the thick foliage.

To ensure there are no stresses during your holiday, each of the villas is assigned a butler to deal with anything and everything, from unpacking the bags to changing the flights home. The personal service is taken to the extent that the butler is the person who serves at your table and delivers room service.

They get to know your wishes, habits and quirks in order to serve you better, but it's a tough job to get it just right and it depends to some extent on every other aspect of the resort functioning perfectly. At this point the butler service of Kanuhura and Soneva Fushi have the edge, partly due to the training and partly due to their years of experience as resorts, perfecting the details. Island Hideaway only opened in late 2005. It has the rates to compare with the top resorts and might reach their heights in time.

Island Hideaway has taken its cue in looks and decor from Soneva Fushi, which to my mind is an excellent way to go. And like an earlier Soneva Fushi it has fewer rooms and the island is less developed. It is appealing for being in a more complete, unaltered state of nature.

The beach is untouched, the sand being wonderfully fine and soft continuously around the crescent-shaped island, with bonus bulges at each end. It is an island thick in screwpine rather than palms but the rooms are set so far apart that total privacy is assured. Bicycles are given with each room, though there are also club carts for speedier transport.

There are six categories of rooms all built in that luxurious rustic style that is so right for Maldives. Every roof is thatched, every wall and column deliberately uneven; the floors are wooden, the textiles are cotton in plain earthy colours.

The differences between the rooms are essentially size - of the rooms, the surrounding enclosure and the pool. The 7 Funa Pavilions (176 sqm) and the 7 Raamba Retreats (385 sqm) don't have pools and have less of a beach in front. The 20 Donakulhi Residences (550 sqm) are in the majority and are perhaps the ideal compromise between price, size and position. The 5 Jasmine

Garden Villas are an enormous 705 sqm with a ten-metre infinity pool and floating dining pavilion connected. With the butler bringing all your meals if you wish, there is no need to leave its confines. The ultimate rooms are the two Hideaway Palaces at 1,420 sqm that sit by the beach bulge and enjoy several infinity pools and eight separate thatched pavilions.

Just off the spa are the final two rooms, called Spa Water Villas. These are 235 sqm and fit in a two-table treatment room, a sauna and a steam room, a bedroom and a separate lounge that opens on two sides to the turquoise lagoon and deeper blues near the horizon.

The spa itself also has two treatment rooms over the water. These are considerably more popular than the land rooms, which are so large as to have redundant space incompatible with the desired intimacy of a top spa setting. It is run by Mandara Spas from Bali, with their wonderful therapists and delightful menu of therapies. The most popular is the Bali full body massage and their signature treatment is the Mandara Massage, which involves two therapists and five different techniques from different traditions.

The whole resort is well set up for families. Most of the rooms are more than large enough, there is a play centre attended by young female staff who also babysit (and the butler, of course, is happy to help), there are kids' meals, a kids' pool, and a large shallow lagoon ideal for swimming and watersports. All unpowered watersports are free of charge, so it's great for families playing together.

Snorkeling is reasonably good and is easily accessed on one side, just off the beach by the big swimming pool. This is actually a narrow channel much used as a short cut by dolphins and many other of the big pelagics, including occasional mantas. Manta season here is between September and January when, at a feeding station 15 minutes away, hundreds at a time have been experienced.

In this channel too is the marina for which Island Hideaway was originally conceived. It is just the spot to tie up your yacht when cruising down the Arabian Sea. Otherwise just fly in, boat across from the regional airport and fall in love with a beautiful resort that is going to get even better.

T 660 6688 F 660 6633
E respgest.kihaad@valtur.it
www.valtur.com

Baa Atoll

 30 mins

$3

$1.50

$2

1/2 $30

$35

Valtur

$98

5 x $440

PADI

Kihaad

Valtur Kihaad has a delightful atmosphere and a great holiday can be had here, despite the quirky built environment.

Kihaad is run entirely by the Italian tour operator Valtur. This is their 'Paradise' category holiday and as such the animation is softer and the day-to-day resort life is quieter and more easygoing than the other Valtur club destinations.

The atmosphere is lovely. The Italian staff members are more than friendly, they are instant friends. There appear to be no rules or barriers beyond the injunction for everyone to get along together and make the magic work. The Maldivian staff, often longstanding and Italian speaking, understand this and play their part admirably.

Ideally the setting would reflect and add to the atmosphere but here it has to be overcome, to some extent. Valtur took over a resort that was already complete, a resort built in a too, too solid and grandiose style. The reception is vast, for no apparent reason, and the restaurant is enclosed and formal, though it is wonderful on the deck outside where naturally everybody likes to be.

The beach rooms have thatch on top and coir rope around the concrete pillars but fail to be attractive and intimate. A fine draped four-poster bed dominates the interior but the decor details, such as outsize 'Greek urn' lamps and a ghetto blaster CD player, are unsettling.

The rooms are large, with a day bed as standard and space for another. The 18 Deluxe rooms differ from the 86 Superior rooms only in having a bathtub/jacuzzi as well as the shower. And, critically, face south on the best beach. The ten Over Water Villas are essentially the same as the beach rooms except for being larger still. The two Over Water Suites are also the same but have double the size, enclosed, with nothing to fill it.

Half the waterbungalows face the sunrise and half the sunset, although a broad walkway around three sides allow guests to move their loungers to suit. A vertical ladder gives access to the large, beautiful, sandy-bottomed lagoon.

For most resorts the layout of the island would be a disaster but here it works. There are two rows of rooms, one behind the other and the majority of them face north, catching little direct sun. The best beach faces south and is fronted by the public area, from the restaurant to the reception and jetty to the swimming pool and bar. What happens is guests stay by their rooms for quiet moments but spend most of the time together, active or inactive, in this area.

Aquagym, volleyball and sunbathing during the day turn to music and aperitifs in the evening, massage or stretching demonstration and cabaret at night. A good swimming pool is surrounded by a broad deck for a pool bar, coffee shop, dance floor and seating, both shaded and open.

The deck outside the restaurant, pierced by illuminated coconut palms and looking out across the wide beach to the lapping waters of the lagoon, is one of the most attractive settings for an evening meal that I have come across. Candlelit and accompanied by a happy hubbub, any meal tastes that much better. Not that the food needs any more help, it is exemplary. Dinners are a mix of set plates, live cooking and a buffet of supplements and alternatives inside.

The resort spa is at the end of its own jetty, at the edge of the public area. It looks somewhat forbidding from the beach - dark and enclosed. But inside, it is a revelation. The five massage rooms, two beauty rooms and large mixed jacuzzi room are all bright and welcoming. Two of the rooms are dedicated to Thai massages and an ayurveda therapist is also part of the staff.

Other facilities seem to be part of a company policy and are mostly inappropriate in Maldives. There is a very large gym, a cavernous hall with badminton and squash courts and an outdoor tennis court, all of which get little use, but they are there if desired.

| 1 | 2 | 3 | 4 | 5 | 6 | 7 | 8 | 9 | 10 |

LOWEST   RELATIVE PRICE   HIGHEST

| 1 | 2 | 3 | 4 | 5 | 6 | 7 | 8 | 9 | 10 |

MOST   ROOM DENSITY   LEAST

T 662 1010 F 662 1011
E info@komandoo.com
www.komandoo.com

Lhaviyani Atoll

 40 mins

 240 mins

 $4.50

 $3

 $3.50

 $55

 $35

ProDivers

 $66

5 x $314

PADI $665

Komandoo

Komandoo has just the simple elements of a Maldives holiday - and the guests want nothing more. For them, this is one of the islands that offer the ideal mix.

It is small, comfortable and quiet; there is no animation and little organised entertainment, but the intimate atmosphere is conducive to mixing and meeting with fellow guests on the same wavelength.

The resort boasts 15 beautiful waterbungalows and 45 land rooms, which sit right on the beach and are identical, except that ten of them have jacuzzis. The other difference is whether the rooms are on the northeast side or the southwest side of the cigar-shaped island. The wide southwest beach has the sun on it just about all day but the rooms on the other beach have a more private look and feel to them, as the vegetation goes down further and the water comes up closer. The sun leaves the northeast beach in the afternoon but you have a sunlit view out over open water to two beautiful desert islands. On the other side, the view is partly obscured by Hinnavaru, an inhabited island. Low walls set out in the lagoon run right around the island, which is disappointing, but they are soon out of mind, especially at high tide when they are also out of sight.

The beach is excellent almost all around, and the rooms have steps directly up from it, except for two or three rooms together in one corner, where the steps emerge from the water. For some guests this is even more exciting. Constructed entirely in Finnish pine, with unfussy matt black metal furniture, the rooms have a crisp Scandinavian look to them. They are warm, yet full of light. Bring your own favourite CDs to play on the midi system or borrow from a large in-house selection. The bathrooms, curving around the back, are also light and well designed. The stand-alone shower is just as it should be.

Snorkeling is excellent because the island is ideally sited in a channel. Although the reef edge slopes away rather than drops off and is not among the best for coral, it is a magnet for a wide range of creatures. One marine biologist from Hamburg counted 265 species without ever going for a dive. Manta rays, eagle rays and dolphins are not infrequent visitors to the reef as they pass on into the atoll.

The dive school positively encourages snorkeling, with equipment, lessons and trips out to the nearby wrecks, thilas and caves (on the Kuredu housereef). Tom and Babs, the very pleasant and supportive base leaders, reckon that if you come to the Maldives you have to put your head under the water and if one partner is into diving then snorkeling is a fine way for the other partner to pass the time and start to understand the obsession.

With a rare concentration of narrow channels one after the other, the diving itself is some of the very best and the most local. There are 15 sites within 15 minutes. The system at the dive base is as easy as the place itself is open and welcoming. With relatively few guests, the attention is personal, and that extends to chats in the bar over problems and preferences (as well, of course, as reliving those diving highs).

The bar is conducive for long, slow evenings. An atmosphere of ease and camaraderie is engendered by its low-slung cosiness and encouraged by the manager or manageress who are, here, the host and hostess. Both in the bar and in the restaurant it's clear to see that people are meeting, greeting and enjoying new friendships.

The restaurant is at its best in the evenings too. Here, the Indian head chef acts as second host, explaining dishes, tickling appetites and setting a tone of bonhomie. The food is very good with plenty of adventure and variety. The setting is perfect: sandy floor, lamp-lit tables under a high thatch roof, low coral walls and wooden deck out to the lagoon. Lunch is also good, though Hinnavaru is visible (and audible with the middaycall to prayer), while breakfast, it must be said, is sparse and ordinary.

As befits the place, there are no boards at reception offering or pushing excursions, entertainments or special dinners. Although all the usual trips are offered, the take-up is not high. A most unusual one is a trip that combines the atoll capital, Naifaru, with the largest tuna processing and canning plant in the country, Felivaru. The most popular is the weekly trip on the sailing cruiser 'Briit'. And the most private is the free launch to Kudadu, a beautiful desert island with excellent snorkeling. A maximum of four people are taken but usually this is just for one couple alone.

A good spa rounds off the possibilities and that's it, a perfect place to do very little.

1	2	3	4	**5**	6	7	8	9	10		1	2	3	4	5	**6**	7	8	9	10
LOWEST		RELATIVE PRICE			HIGHEST						MOST			ROOM DENSITY				LEAST		

T 666 0527 F 666 0556
E sales@unient.com.mv
www.universalresorts.com

Rasdhoo Atoll

 20 mins

 105 mins

 $4.15

 $3.65

 $4.40

 $48

Rasdhoo Atoll Divers

$60

5 x $285

PADI $555

Kuramathi

Kuramathi is the only island in the country with more than one resort: there are three here.

They are the 'economy class' Village at one end, the 'business class' Cottage Club in the narrowing middle, and the 'first class' Blue Lagoon at the tip. The long island and clear divisions allow for very different holiday experiences at the same time in different places. Nonetheless, movement up and down the island is encouraged with open access to all bars and specialty restaurants and the shared sports, swimming pool and spa area in the middle. Movement is aided by pleasant paths and a free minivan on call.

Having graded the resorts using airline terminology, on closer inspection the picture is less clear-cut. The new Deluxe Rooms on Village, for example, are a class above the resort's standard rooms and its ordinary bar and lounge. By contrast, on Blue Lagoon, the unchanged Beach Bungalows, with their obstructed views, strain to be categorized as first class. Then again, there's a clear programme of rolling improvements all over the island and the food and beverage set-up, in particular, is becoming impressive.

The guests on Village tend to be younger and livelier than on the other two resorts. Almost everyone is on an all-inclusive package and the bar rocks in the evening, despite the unsympathetic tiled floors and odd levels. Cottage Club, with its many waterbungalows and cocooned public area, is usually the quietest of the three. Blue Lagoon, upmarket but mostly all-inclusive, has a reputation for action on its set entertainment nights.

Each resort has its own dive centre (and all three share a Marine Biological Station, which is good to see). The nearby diving highlights are the unique hammerhead shark point, a manta point and several caves. Further afield are the renowned thilas of northeast Ari Atoll, which are combined in double tank and all-day dives.

The Village has three categories of rooms, of which Deluxe account for over half. These are excellent modern rooms with attractive bathrooms, set in semi-circles behind the best section of beach. Because of this, it can be relatively densely populated in this area. The other side of the island is the quieter side and

faces south. The beaches can be very narrow here though and the rooms are the Superiors or Standards. The Standard room seems basic now and the Superior rather old-fashioned, but they both serve their purposes well enough.

As the Village becomes the Cottage Club and Spa, white sand is suddenly spread thickly over the path and the Beach Bungalows earn more space. Tiled with terracotta in the bedrooms and stylish black slate in the bathrooms, with white walls and coconut wood furnishings, these are, again, good modern rooms. The waterbungalows have been around a while but are still attractive with their polygon shape, woven mat interiors, large windows and generous balconies. The reef drop-off and good snorkeling are just a short swim away.

The reception, bar and lounge area of Cottage is the most attractive of the three. A waft of incense drifts through the cool, thatched interior and out to a quiet courtyard with 'found' boatyard sculptures. In contrast to this private elegance, the nearby swimming pool, spa and sports centre, all in great order, are where everyone comes to play. Village guests must pay for the privilege but all-in packages are reasonable.

Perhaps in an effort to make the public area of the Blue Lagoon more prestigious, the final effect is less 'of a piece' than Cottage's equivalent. There are six or seven types of flooring and four types of chairs and tables, for example. But the lighting and atmosphere are good in the evening. A large gazebo over the water is for special dinners in the night and sunbathing during the day. The beaches at this narrow end of the island are narrow themselves, with the vegetation often getting down to the water's edge. This is unfortunately true of several of the Beach Bungalows, which also look over a line of coral walls in the water.

At the tip of the island is a slender sandbank meandering off westward - ideal for a long, romantic stroll at sunset. With a plethora of colourful flowers and carefully tended shrubbery around sandy paths, Blue Lagoon does have a romantic setting. Indeed the whole island is unified by a luxuriant combination of mature, natural vegetation and managed floral decoration. For all those looking for choice and variety on a largish island, Kuramathi has to be a strong contender.

| 1 | 2 | 3 | 4 | 5 | 6 | 7 | 8 | 9 | 10 | | 1 | 2 | 3 | 4 | 5 | 6 | 7 | 8 | 9 | 10 |

LOWEST　RELATIVE PRICE　HIGHEST　　MOST　　ROOM DENSITY　　LEAST

T 662 0337　F 662 0332
E info@kuredu.com
www.kuredu.com

Lhaviyani Atoll

 40 mins

 240 mins

 $4.50

 $3

 $3.50

 $55

 $28

 ProDivers

$61

5 x $295

PADI $595

Kuredu

Kuredu was once young and brash, but as the years passed the changes came and it matured into the complete item, a beautiful resort for all types and all budgets.

As this is the third largest resort island, space was available to build a separate up-market mini-resort in a quiet corner. Named 'Sangu', it occupies the west tip, or the tail end of this whale shark shaped island. There is no need for Sangu guests to move from their own reception, bar and restaurant - beautifully constructed of thatch and re-used coral (it is now illegal to build with new coral). Or from their powder sand beach that stretches away and fades into the sunset. If all you require is beach and sea and peace and quiet in a conducive setting then this may do very nicely.

The most expensive rooms are the Over Water Suites, followed by the Water Villas. All are within swimming distance of the reef drop-off and excellent snorkeling. Inevitably the Suites, at the end of the line, are best positioned for the sunset. The others, facing north-west, have a little more acute views. If direct sun and immediate access to sand is more important than being over the water and accessible to the reef, then the Jacuzzi Beach Villas, on the south side, are the ones to go for.

The beach on this side, facing into the atoll, is the longest, widest stretch of glorious sand that any resort can boast of. And that's some boast. Enjoying it, beyond Sangu's Jacuzzi Beach Villas, are all the regular Kuredu Beach Villas. The main public area is suitably placed right in the middle of the stretch. Here the more gregarious guests can be found around the pool and the pool bar, milling around the reception and its own bar and volleyball court, or in the shallows trying out some watersports.

The last few years have seen a considerable upgrading of facilities and all-round standards here, with its consequent increase in price and average age of guest. It hasn't stopped the fun by any means but now there's a lot more to do than just party. The watersports centre is the biggest and probably the most active in the country. Good reasons for this are the free canoes and windsurfers (after a three-hour course for novices) and the free introduction to windsurfing, catamaran sailing and kiteboarding three times a week. Then there is the whole gamut of motorboat drawn sports: waterskiing, wakeboarding, tubes, blasts and banana.

Another 'biggest in the country' is the impressive dive base. Well thought through and very well equipped, it is run not only with apparent professionalism but with an easy cameraderie that belies the complexity of all the activities. Guests range from hard-core, single-minded divers who really know what they want, down to the anxious and uncertain first-timers. But this doesn't seem to cause a hiccup in the system. There are enough instructors, boats and dive sites to keep everyone satisfied.

The dive centre really does the snorkeling properly too. A good practice that some other resorts, especially the larger ones, would do well to pick up on. A separate board with an introduction and lots of information, details the options and activities. Daily lessons are free, as are the accompanied snorkels from the beach on the excellent housereef. On top of this are regular half-day and full-day snorkel trips with the guests well prepared as to what there is to enjoy.

The north side of the island faces the open sea so, as is always the case, there is a problem retaining a decent beach. Groynes and sea walls do the job and there are a few areas of soft sand but mostly it's not so very pretty. The rooms on this side are the Beach Bungalows and as a tip, the lower the number the better the setting. These rooms are numbered in the 400s and 300s and from 315 down you would get, for the cheapest prices, a quiet, private, natural environment with your own little beach and the closest distance to the reef drop-off.

Taking the boat transfer from the airport and booking into a Beach Bungalow or taking the seaplane and booking into a Sangu Over Water Suite are two very different ways of doing Kuredu. Not only does the resort accommodate differing budgets but it also allows you to relax in private for days on end or stay constantly active. Another bonus is a six-hole golf course and driving range. Although this may sound horribly inappropriate, it really works. Certainly it is helped by the fact that it is so well hidden inside the island that you would walk straight past it if you didn't know it was there. It is insidiously addictive and there's even a tiny country club style 'seventh hole'.

1	2	3	4	5	6	**7**	8	9	10
LOWEST		RELATIVE PRICE			HIGHEST				

1	2	3	4	5	6	7	8	9	10
MOST			ROOM DENSITY				LEAST		

T 664 2324 F 664 3885
E sales@unient.com.mv
www.universalresorts.com

North Male Atoll

 8 mins

 20 mins

 $5.50

 $4.40

 $5.50

 $65

 $38

 Eurodivers

 $71

5 x $322

 PADI $539

Kurumba

Kurumba has a historic place in the amazing story of Maldives tourism. It was the very first resort to be opened, in 1972.

Back then guests were happy to make do with very simple small rooms, without a/c or fresh water, and a diet of fish, bananas and rice. Since then, like an evolution tree, the resorts have developed rapidly and branched off in different (but always upward) directions.

As the closest resort to the capital and the airport, Kurumba has always had, as it were, a licence to develop differently, as a mix of natural Maldives and a prestigious showcase of modern Maldives that could host visiting presidents and business executives. After a total remake in 2003/4, Kurumba today is a five-star, compact, planned 'village' that offers options in living, dining and playing for everyone from princes to sun-loving, (fairly wealthy) conventional tourists.

Like a new, planned village, there isn't a single path circling the island but a network of them connecting all the rooms and facilities together and shared by pedestrians and cars. Well, no, that's really strolling couples and humming club cars. The seven room categories are in distinct locations and they cluster in shapes like horseshoes and candelabras around gardens. The village square (with piped music instead of a public address) is the paved area around the swimming pool, which is surrounded by the restaurants, bars and lounges that vaguely mark the time within each long, sun-drenched day.

The entire island is surrounded by a very good beach that narrows and bulges in different places as it moves throughout the year, unrestricted by groynes. This fine feature is, however, somewhat offset by the presence of a lagoon wall that encircles the resort. After a couple of days it slips from the mind, except where it is close to land.

It is an odd fact that the wall is closest to land just by the most expensive rooms. Here, too, the view is over to the continuing extension of the airport island. In any case, few people reading this are likely to be eyeing up the four Presidential Suites or the Royal Kurumba Residence, with their no expense spared interiors of gold taps and Persian carpets.

The lowest category rooms, the 38 Superior Rooms are larger than the next category up, the 39 Deluxe Rooms, but are in blocks of four and look out to Male and the airport. They are, however, excellent rooms, as are all the rooms on the new Kurumba. As a rule all the rooms are large and attractively modern, with impressive bathrooms and fitted throughout with top quality furniture, furnishings and amenities.

The 74 Deluxe Bungalows are the same size as the superiors but are detached and have a few quality improvements. Importantly, they have some of the best beach and look out to the quiet, relatively empty horizons to the west and north. The other two categories, Private Villas (16) and Pool Villas (8) are on either side of the top rooms mentioned above - except that four of the pool villas are part of a 'close' of deluxe bungalows and ten of the private villas are behind the others.

The options for accommodation are matched by the choices for dining. Apart from the all-day coffee shop and the poolside pizzeria, there are seven separate restaurants - the main one, a grill, an Arabic, an Italian, an Indian, a Chinese and a Japanese. There is no questioning the effort and success in making the specialist restaurants into convincing settings. It is all excellent theatre (down to the Arabic hookahs). As most guests are on bed and breakfast deals, they are encouraged to have a different country experience every couple of nights.

Indulgence is a good part of the story here, from the accommodation to the cuisine and the spa experience. The Per Aquum Spa is among the best in the country - beautifully designed and inclusive of everything one could want to feel utterly spoilt.

Indulging themselves on Kurumba are the usual mix of Japanese, British (25%), Germans (25%) and other Europeans, as well as a new mix of Russians (25%) and Chinese. With a new Kids' Club, it is also particularly welcoming to families.

Diving in the region is good and well established but the housereef snorkeling will take a long time to get back to its best after the major reconstruction. The watersports centre is one of the top centres in the country, well run and comprehensively equipped. It's what you can say about Kurumba as a whole.

1	2	3	4	5	**6**	7	8	9	10

LOWEST   RELATIVE PRICE   HIGHEST

1	**2**	3	4	5	6	7	8	9	10

MOST   ROOM DENSITY   LEAST

T 664 3042 F 664 3041
E sales@unient.com.mv
www.universalresorts.com

South Male Atoll

  20 mins

 55 mins

 $4.40

 $3.30

 $3.85

 $61

 $25

 Laguna

 $52

6 x $297

PADI $687

Laguna

Laguna has had some great changes over the last couple of years. Today the resort is exciting, handsome and well run.

The rooms have been completely renewed, the cuisine transformed and good things have been happening with personnel and training. You pay more for your holiday here these days but you get much more too.

The 65 Deluxe Rooms are smaller than the 48 Deluxe Bungalows and are mostly in blocks of four (two up and two down) but both types are now beautifully modern and well appointed. Though not exactly minimalist, there are no fussy design elements. The rooms now seem to flow from the raised four-poster bed platform down through the simple but elegant sitting area and out the front to the beach.

That flow is evident in the newly refurbished 17 Water Suites too. Large, light and white, though never 'cold', the rooms draw you out to the extended wooden decks and the lagoon beyond. The housereef is not accessible but the snorkeling within the lagoon here is good. There is no question that these are top class rooms.

There are two other rooms, which may increase in number depending on their popularity. One is called a Pool Villa and one a Jacuzzi Villa. These are the resort's premium rooms. They bear a resemblance to the excellent new Hilton rooms: long from front to back, running from the raised four-poster in the glass, wood and white bedroom, past the sunken bath and out to a private pool, a garden and small pergola with daybed.

All the rooms are pretty close together as this is not a sparsely populated resort, but still the privacy is good because of the impressive flowering of plants in front and all around the rooms. The colours and variety of plants certainly lift the resort visually but it doesn't look too manicured.

It is indicative of the new Laguna that the old concrete path that ran close to the rooms all the way around the island has now disappeared under soft white sand and guests walk further away from the rooms. It is still the case that no careful choice of room or request to move is necessary because of the beach, which is fairly consistent all the way around.

The reception, main bar and restaurant are the same somewhat formal, 'hard-edged' buildings, but modern interior redesign of the restaurant and coffee shop has made those areas very attractive. And even more attractive is the overall quality of the cuisine here.

Under the guidance of an Australian, formerly Swiss, executive chef, Dominique, the coffee shop, just for an example, offers seafood fondue in the evenings (the only one in the country for sure) as well as adventurous meals with Ostrich and Kangaroo. And a great innovation is the offering of deals to use half-board packages for breakfast and lunch, leaving the choice of where to go for the evening meal in any of the specialty restaurants.

In the main restaurant three dinners are buffet and four are set plate (with three choices) served at the table. The specialty restaurants, apart from the excellent coffee shop, are a Mediterranean, an Asian and a perfectly placed Grill for candlelit dinners on the best beach of all.

There is an interestingly shaped swimming pool, with a large deck and small children's pool, near to the main bar but, perhaps because the beach and lagoon are so good all around, it's never crowded.

Generally speaking this isn't a 'stay up dancing and drinking all night' place nor an 'always go to bed early' place. There's a separate small, cool Karaoke lounge if it takes your fancy but it isn't heavily used. Daytime entertainments are more popular, including big game fishing, a Male excursion and various snorkeling trips.

One of the snorkeling options is a boat out to the resort's own housereef. The reef is just about reachable from the beach by swimming but guests are asked not to do this because of a potentially fast channel current. Snorkeling, then, is a bit of a disappointment, but, on the other hand, I can hardly exaggerate how good the dive school is.

Herbert Unger and his partner Petra are two of those few who have been in Maldives since practically the beginning of tourism here. Their experience is equaled by just a couple of others in the country and they run a superb set-up on Laguna. Every diving guest has his or her name on their basket, their weights and their tank. The equipment is sorted out, loaded, retrieved from the boat, rinsed and hung up by the crew. The diver just dives. With access to the renowned sites of the southern part of North Male Atoll as well as those of South Male Atoll, the variety of dive sites as well as the service are what bring the guests back to this centre year after year.

1	2	3	4	**5**	6	7	8	9	10		1	2	**3**	4	5	6	7	8	9	10

LOWEST · RELATIVE PRICE · HIGHEST · MOST · ROOM DENSITY · LEAST

T 668 0013 F 668 0646
E info@lilybeachmaldives.com
www.lilybeachmaldives.com

South Ari Atoll

 25 mins

 inc

 inc

 inc

$36

$19

Ocean Pro

$65

5 x $325

PADI $619

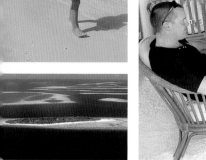

Lily Beach

This is one of the resorts that gets better and better. It has a devoted following for reasons which might not be immediately obvious but which gradually become very clear.

As a well-priced, all-inclusive destination it is one of the very best in the country. A clear, comprehensive in-room directory settles the guests and gives them confidence that this is a well-organised set-up.

It is refreshing to read that the de-salinated water is safe to drink. It always is but most resorts don't advertise this fact. Bottles of mineral water are still available for free. And there is a great deal more included for free that is often not included in other places. All watersports are free (although there are no mechanised watersports), the good floodlit tennis court is too, and the gym, the table tennis and full-sized snooker table. Plus all the necessary snorkeling equipment is given out with compliments for the duration of your holiday.

What can't be given away or bought at any price is friendliness and this place has a friendly atmosphere, set by all the members of staff, particularly the waiters, bar staff and room boys. It makes a big, big difference to a place.

The whole built environment is spick and span, the level of maintenance being right up there with the best. The green on green colour scheme in a solid, straight-lined setting won't be to everyone's taste, but the sand on the floors throughout mixes the formality with the informality of bare feet.

All three meals are generous buffets and teatime snacks at the pool bar differ every day. For a change there are various options of private dinners on the beach and on an uninhabited island. The excursion list is a long one from sunrise excursion to sunset fishing and barbecue. Island visits as a group and privately and various fishing and snorkeling trips are also offered.

The varied snorkeling trips are popular despite Lily Beach having its own nearby reef with ten cut-throughs. The housereef snorkeling is quite good but the current is often strong in the high season as the island lies in the middle of a channel.

Ocean Pro runs the dive school and this region of South Ari has many renowned sites, although a good number of them call for experience, owing to the nature of thila dives in the channels. What you save on the holiday you might be willing to spend on a Maldives diving treat or two.

There is good spacing between the tables in the bars and restaurant and no waiting for the sports and other activities as there are not nearly as many rooms on the resort as there might be. Just 85 in all. On the south side of this thin, east-west laying island are just the 16 Semi-Water Bungalows and five of the 68 Superior Rooms. On the other side of the island are the remaining Superior Rooms and the one Suite (over-the-top).

The Semi-Water Bungalows are entered from the land and, on the other side, have steps down to the narrow lagoon. These are large, spotless, well-appointed rooms in the resort's green on green scheme. As with the Superior Rooms, they are not cosy but you couldn't find anything to complain about. Unusually, every room has a CD player and hairdryer.

The Semi-Water Bungalows are just ten metres away from the reef drop-off, which is great for a drift snorkel, but the downside is that there is little beach on this side. For this reason there is a lagoon wall all the way along, which is very neatly done but unfortunate nonetheless.

The lagoon wall bends around one tip and goes down a third of the other side. Where the wall stops is where the beach finally comes into its own. These are the best rooms to have and, inevitably, they are booked out most the year round by return guests who know how it is.

The beach, then, is the one issue on this resort (plus the retaining lagoon wall). You might get to love the decor but even if you don't I bet you would get to love the resort as a whole. It is a sorted, friendly, excellent value-for-money all-inclusive.

1	2	3	4	5	6	7	8	9	10
LOWEST   RELATIVE PRICE   HIGHEST

1	2	3	4	5	6	7	8	9	10
MOST   ROOM DENSITY   LEAST

T 668 0596 F 668 0524
E club@maafushivaru.com.mv

South Ari Atoll

✈ 25 mins

🍺 $3.85

💧 $3.30

🥤 $3.30

🌴 $50

🎣 $20

▮◤ The Sea
Dragon

🤿 $61

6 x 🤿 $341

PADI $745

Maafushivaru

Maafushivaru T Club, to give its full name, is operated by Turisanda and is entirely Italian.

The resort, formerly known as Twin Island, had always been Italian but now, after a complete rebuild, it has moved up to the top rung. It looks stunning, feels classy and comfortable and delivers a great Maldives holiday.

The country has taken a long while to find the right resort style to express itself, something true to its history and unique setting. This resort is a great example of the new thinking and the new way forward. Not insignificantly, it was designed down to its smallest detail by a Maldivian.

In many ways the new style is a reflection of how it used to be at the beginning of tourism here: thatch on the roof, sand on the floor, woven matting and plenty of wood, including coconut wood. The walls are minimal, affording sightlines through to the beach and water. And at the same time, it is now absolutely modern, with quality fixtures and fittings and luxury interior decor in tans, cream and ivory.

What makes Maafushivaru particularly special, design-wise, are the specific Maldives references. The buffet table is a close copy of the decorative coral base of Hukuru Miski, the historic Friday Mosque in Male. And the dishes rest atop small Thundu Kunaa, the unique Maldives reed mats. A single line of coral decorates the exterior room walls, while inside every room the plastering is carefully laid to echo the look of a full coral wall.

The waterbungalows are simply beautiful. Apart from those 'coral walls' everything is of either wood or glass. Two sides are floor to ceiling windows and glass doors, bathing the room in light. But with the blinds drawn down, the spot lighting lit and the designer CD player on, it's a cosy heaven. A wardrobe and dressing room (with a Pininfarina Lavazza Blue Ultimat Espresso machine!) leads to a light and very stylish bathroom and shower, which itself leads through to the sundeck. The ten bungalows facing southwest get more sunshine on the decks than the ten facing northeast.

The Beach Villas are a little smaller and less glamorous but each has the bonus of a large verandah looking out to the beach and lagoon. Very unusually, this is a triangular shaped island with the public buildings and the first five rooms on the one side without a decent beach and with a sea wall. The other two sides have a wide and fine-grained beach leading to a sandy lagoon of a good swimming depth.

During the day much of the life of the resort happens on the beach in front of the swimming pool and beach bar. And similarly in the evening, after dinner, the beach bar becomes the cabaret theatre, with seating flowing back through the pillars of the open sides to the swimming pool deck. The pool now sparkles in the dark with coloured stars, as it's lit from beneath with fibre optic spots.

The prominent spa faces the main beach one way and, the other side of the treatment rooms, clear out to the horizon. It is exceptionally well equipped and offers a wide array of treatments from Indian and Thai massages to head, shoulder and neck work, manicure and pedicures, body wraps and hair and beauty treatments. The masseuses are from Thailand and Kerala, while the beautician is European.

There is a decent extent of snorkeling along the reef and the quality is good but not exceptional. The dive school is located on its own jetty and has the luxury to choose from a large number of excellent nearby sites, as this is the renowned area of southeast Ari Atoll.

If I could find fault at all with this gorgeous resort, it would be that the food did not quite hit the heights that one might expect from an Italian five-star establishment. But, with a five-star management on the job, that might not be the case any longer.

T 666 0588 F 666 0568
E maaya@dhivehinet.net.mv

1	2	3	4	5	6	7	8	9	10
LOWEST		RELATIVE PRICE		HIGHEST					

1	2	3	4	5	6	7	8	9	10
MOST			ROOM DENSITY			LEAST			

North Ari Atoll

 24 mins

 inc

 inc

 $33

 $10

Maayafushi

$52

5 x $255

PADI $485

Maayafushi

First impressions of Maayafushi are not good. It wouldn't win any style or beauty competitions. But just give the place a day or two and you'll probably find yourself seduced by its personality.

To describe a place as easygoing and relaxed is commonplace and for almost all resorts it's true to some extent - but Maayafushi is its epitome. Here there are no pretensions, no regulations, no competition and no complaints. On an ideal resort tick list there would be several key boxes unchecked, but Maayafushi's friendliness seems to make that irrelevant. As one happy guy said to me, "Can't fault it".

Prominent groynes march down one side of the island but these have not done their job and so a wall has been built, around half the island (but only in front of a third of the rooms). The circular ends of the groynes prove useful as sunbathing spots in the afternoon, when many of the rooms, facing east, are in the shade. They also double up as a candlelit dinner location (good prices for lobster and seafood).

Although many of the rooms don't have much in the way of a beach, one huge, soft sand spit makes up for it. With the watersports hut at one end playing music, this is a busy, genial area during the day, and a reverentially quiet one at sunset when everyone comes together to watch and photograph.

The resort clientele changed from predominantly German divers to all Italian clubbers and is now a mix of German speakers and British with still around one third Italians. There are evening entertainments in the bar as well as aqua aerobics and some games on the beach but these club activities now take a back seat to the main business of sunbathing, eating and drinking. And diving and snorkeling.

Maayafushi is a good snorkeling island. The drop-off is no more than 60 metres away around half the island. And access channels have been cut at the beginning, the middle and the end of the snorkeling zone. The coral and fish life are abundant, which is not too surprising as this area of North Ari Atoll is world renowned for its dive sites.

Diving interest on Maayafushi is growing again, as it should. The dive school is large and prominent at the end of the jetty next to the reception and the staff is as friendly and helpful as everyone else. Most importantly the diving itself is truly excellent.

The dive school is not as busy as it could be because everyone here is on all-inclusive which generally means less spare money around. There are also many Italians, who tend not to do much diving, and many honeymooners, with shallow pockets and other things on their mind.

The food is unexpectedly good - a three-course mix of buffet and set plates with cold white wine and beer on tap. Again, it is the Italian guests who are probably to thank for this.

The 76 rooms are divided up into 60 Beach Bungalows, 16 Standard Rooms and 7 VIP Rooms. The Standard are just the same as the Bungalows except they are in two-storey blocks and the bathroom is entirely enclosed. The furniture in the rooms is cheap but everything is very clean and well maintained.

The VIP rooms are inside the island behind high walls. This obviously gives them great privacy but no views. The rooms are bigger, the furniture better and there is a swing in the small private garden. Beach access might be an issue on another resort, but because this is such a friendly, unstuffy place there's no problem mixing in and finding a spare sunlounger.

So there it is, a relatively cheap holiday with great staff, good food and idyllic location. You can put up with a lot for that.

T 666 0581 F 666 0554
E madoogali@dhivehinet.net.mv
www.skorpiontravel.com

1	2	3	4	**5**	6	7	8	9	10
LOWEST		RELATIVE PRICE		HIGHEST					

1	2	3	4	5	6	7	**8**	9	10
MOST			ROOM DENSITY				LEAST		

North Ari Atoll

 20 mins

120 mins

$4

$4

$6

$33

$18

Madoogali

$60

7 x   392

PADI $350

Madoogali

Madoogali is a gem of a resort and, in many ways, a model for other islands.

It is as natural looking and as 'green' as a resort can be, yet still as smart and well ordered as the day it opened. Add a first class beach and reef plus outstanding service and you have a winner.

The island is a rare mix of untouched, lush vegetation and areas of tamed nature. A sandy path in front of the rooms is shaded by bowers of bougainvillea, mature palms and more than one very fine banyan tree; while a neat garden marks the crossing of the two interior paths. The rest of the interior is left more or less wild.

Past managers have instigated a number of environmentally friendly procedures. One is to regularly clean the housereef manually, another is disposing of all refuse in the most appropriate manner and recycling whatever is possible (for example, coconut husks and oil drums to local islanders, and kitchen waste turned into fertiliser).

The thick, cream coloured beach has been allowed to flow around the island from season to season as it has always done. The only intervention is temporary sandbagging at the last possible moment. There are no groynes or lagoon walls. This is still a picture perfect island.

The commitment to nature is paralleled by a commitment to maintain the built environment as new. First constructed in 1989, the rooms and public buildings are in perfect shape.

The 50 individual bungalows are solidly made of coral and handsomely decorated inside and out. They are perhaps not as big as they look from outside (with their overhanging thatch) but there is plenty of space for dressing and sitting areas.

The restaurant, bar and reception are sensibly joined together in one area. The bar is the least attractive part for me: simple cane chairs sit on a tiled floor with patches of circular straw mats. The restaurant too looks a little old-fashioned but the happy hubbub at mealtimes tells me the clientele are content and the food is good. The waiters contribute their part. To a man they are excellent - attentive and smiling. Indeed the same is true of all the staff here, most of whom have been here for many years and love the place as much as their guests.

This is predominantly an Italian island but not exclusively. The animation is moderate and there is no pressure to join in. Nonetheless, other Europeans should be happy to go along with the hip, young Italian animators in their blue tops and white shorts and not miss out on some good excursions.

The resort makes good use of a neighbouring desert island - for a picnic lunch on a full-day excursion, for a sunset and sangria event and for private dinners and even overnights. Every day there is a snorkel trip to one of several different reefs as well as a weekly night snorkeling adventure. The resort also runs a successful trawler fishing boat with a history of big catches of sail fin and even giant grouper.

Snorkeling is very good on the housereef too, with much better than average coral life. There is a cut-through on either side of the island but the reef is accessible everywhere at high tide. The dive school runs guided snorkeling and diving on the housereef, as well as courses. The base leader, Christian, a Swiss Italian, has been gaining an enviable reputation by word of mouth from satisfied guests and the diving has greatly increased in popularity. The boats are never crowded, the instructor to diver ratio is high and the overall personal service is much appreciated.

A mention should also be made of the two fine spas. The larger one is inside the island (next to the garden), with space for 'Adam and Eve' treatments (couples together), while the small spa hut is near the water's edge for the added dimension of the soothing sound of the waves upon the shore.

Put simply, Madoogali is still one of the very best Italian resorts in the country.

| 1 | 2 | 3 | **4** | 5 | 6 | 7 | 8 | 9 | 10 |
| LOWEST | | RELATIVE PRICE | | HIGHEST | | | | | |

MOST | 1 | 2 | 3 | 4 | 5 | **6** | 7 | 8 | 9 | 10 | LEAST
ROOM DENSITY

T 664 3157 F 664 5939
E reservations@meeru.com
www.meeru.com

North Male Atoll

60 mins

 $3.85

$1.95

 $4.40

 $45

$15

Ocean Pro

$65

6 x $325

PADI $619

The couple first came here when there were just a few simple rooms reached by two winding paths through the thick undergrowth.

They are still coming back to a resort that has changed beyond all recognition. The reasons were hard to put into words but were summed up with, "It's addictive, this place". In the meantime many more have succumbed to the addiction, with the result that Meeru satisfies more people per annum than just about any other resort.

Perhaps Meeru can be best summed up with the phrase 'affordable dreams'. The big, happy resort has a hundred ways to fulfill a hundred different wishes and expectations. From the fully active party couple to the privacy seeker and from the splurging couple to the careful couple, Meeru seems to deliver on so many people's dreams.

That is not easy to do, of course. The island is the resort base of probably the best group of resorts in the country. The management is always out there, looking, thinking and improving. You can almost feel the place fizzing with activity and ideas.

The latest (and yes, possibly, greatest) idea was the making of a new resort within the resort. Meeru Village is a combination of the existing land-based Water Villas and Jacuzzi Villas with the all-new Jacuzzi Water Villas and over-the-water Spa that stretch out into the lagoon on separate piers. The Village has its own beautiful centre, housing the reception, restaurant and bar, surrounded by a wide, white beach.

No question, the new place is terrific and will swell the ranks of returning Meeru aficionados. Life at the top of the island (the Village takes over the northern end) is classy, comfortable and stylish. It's also quiet as no children are allowed, except as daytime visitors.

The top rooms, the 30 Jacuzzi Water Villas, would not be out of place in a five-star resort. They face either east or west, are very large and unquestionably luxurious. The 27 Water Villas are actually only half over the water and, facing east, don't get sun in the afternoon, but the interiors are quality. Although there is no beach or snorkeling here, it's not far to stroll to the fine bulb of sand at the tip of the island, where there are also some corals and fish.

Trying out an alternative room category is encouraged on this big and varied island, where different rooms in different locations can give different holiday experiences. There is always something to do or something going on throughout the day and into the night but it is never pushed at the guests - no one is ever dragged onto the dance floor or onto the beach volleyball court.

Importantly, every room has a complete catalogue of what there is to do throughout the holiday. A long list of excursions includes a full-day cruise on a sailing yacht (called the Love Boat), a sunset dolphin watch and a Male shopping and sightseeing trip. Daytime resort activities include water polo, tennis, badminton, golf driving and a first class gym. Your evenings might be filled with disco dancing, crab racing, Boduberu, a table tennis tournament or sipping cocktails and making new friends in one of the five bars on the island. At the spa, you can learn to massage your partner for further treats back home.

Apart from the eastern side where the water villas and a few land villas are, you can be assured of a good to excellent beach outside your room. And apart from one area with sea grass, the lagoon is almost perfect - crystal clear water and a sandy bottom.

There are some coral blocks (natural and man-enhanced) in the lagoon that afford some snorkeling, but this is really one of the only areas where the resort is disappointing. A boat is put on every day to take guests to the housereef but you must pay for this and it's not a great reef. The dive centre organises snorkeling trips to better reefs.

Diving is less important to the resort than it used to be but it is still a major draw for many guests. It is a great dive school - managing to be very welcoming and friendly while remaining 100% professional, with an emphasis on safety and no surprises. Guests with no experience at all, including children, can do simple introductory courses, while other guests with hundreds of dives can fulfill their desires with multiple tank, night and full-day diving. With more than 50 sites carefully catalogued, every variation of dive is possible.

The food has greatly improved over the years and is now very hard to fault. One gripe that some guests have is that there are a lot of niggling, unexpected charges, even for all-inclusive guests. If you are aware of this and act accordingly then nothing should stop you having a great holiday on Meeru, and coming back to repeat the treat again and again.

| 1 | 2 | 3 | 4 | 5 | 6 | **7** | 8 | 9 | 10 | | 1 | 2 | 3 | 4 | 5 | **6** | 7 | 8 | 9 | 10 |
LOWEST   RELATIVE PRICE   HIGHEST   MOST   ROOM DENSITY   LEAST

T 668 0500 F 668 0501
E info@mirihi.com
www.mirihi.com

South Ari Atoll

 25 mins

 120 mins

 $4.95

$4.40

$6.60

$71.50

Ocean Pro

$66

5 x $330

PADI $619

Mirihi

In the ever-developing world of Maldives tourism, Mirihi has been reconstructed and re-presented as a five-star boutique resort.

A winning combination of a casual setting with stylish decor and amicable staff maintaining very high standards, not to mention great snorkeling and diving, now mark this out as one of the very best small resorts in the country.

In keeping with the newly fashionable original Maldives look, all the roofs are thatched, there's sand on the floor throughout and daylight floods in. With the prominent use of quality timber, and furnishings in ivory, whites and tans the effect is at once calming and uplifting.

In terms of service and attitude, something even more imaginative is attempted here, a sort of 'grown-up hospitality', a give and take of respect and trust. Not signing for bills at all might make a reappearance but it is at least discreet and infrequent. There are no designated seats in the restaurant, guests are free to drop into the staff area, free to pick up CDs at the reception, free to take out any watersports equipment. It is indicative that each room is individually named (for native trees and flowers) rather than just numbered. The names of the occupants are discreetly displayed alongside.

European, Japanese and Maldivian staff, a good number of them female, deliver an impressive standard of service. They are clearly well trained and motivated. The same must be true of the chefs for the food is sumptuous. The lunch and dinner buffets are inventive, thoughtfully put together and delicious. Thursday, for example, is the Japanese and Vietnamese night, while Saturday it's Malaysian and Thai.

If that wasn't enough, there's a specialty restaurant over the water that just demands to be tried out. The Muraka serves 'surf and turf' haute cuisine in a modern, seductive environment. And once a week, with seating limited to 16, puts on an extra special multi-course meal with matching wines presented by their Master of Wine.

The pleasures of this resort are mostly of the romantic, quiet variety. Even the excursions tend that way, with a Castaway trip to a desert island and Champagne Breakfast on a sandbank. If you haven't come on your honeymoon here, as many

do, you might come to renew your wedding vows in a specially organised ceremony with local touches. Whatever the situation you should be looking for a completely relaxing and quiet holiday because that is what you will certainly get. There are no evening entertainments on any night.

Understandably there are no motored watersports on offer, but for the free catamaran and windsurfing there's a large sandy lagoon off one end of the island, which is ideal. The snorkeling area is not extensive but what there is is very rewarding. The coral life is far better than most resorts and the fish life is abundant. There are also no strong currents to be concerned about.

Perhaps as a spillover from the good snorkeling, and also from the prominent position of the building, the dive school seems to tick over all day with lessons, housereef diving and boat trips. Mirihi is very fortunate with its location within easy reach of one of the best Manta Points in the country, some of the best thila dives and also the outside sites where whale sharks are tracked.

There is a lovely, big beach outside the reception and main bar, at its peak during the high season. The problem is that isn't where it's needed. The north end of the island, which has 16 Water Villas off it, develops a beach during the southwest monsoon (off season) but very little during the northeast (high season). There is a decent beach behind the Water Villas on the west side but the rooms then interrupt the view. The six Beach Rooms do have some permanent beach. Having said all that, the island is so small that it's only ever a couple of minutes to find your place in the sun.

The rooms themselves are predictably beautiful. Wood is used throughout; beautifully crafted wood, with satisfying variations in colour and finish. An original painting hangs above each bed, complementing the artfully designed and expensively furnished rooms. The decks are generous and might face west, north or east depending on which room you have. You'll have to return to get your favourite; they each have something special going for them.

Mirihi itself has a great deal that is special about it. There is no question about its arrival in the top bracket.

| 1 | 2 | 3 | 4 | **5** | 6 | 7 | 8 | 9 | 10 | | 1 | 2 | **3** | 4 | 5 | 6 | 7 | 8 | 9 | 10 |

LOWEST   RELATIVE PRICE   HIGHEST   MOST   ROOM DENSITY   LEAST

T 668 0517   F 668 0509
E info@moofushi.com
www.moofushi.com

South Ari Atoll

 25 mins

$4

$3

$6

$30

$15

Moofushi

 $73

6 x $420

PADI $530

Moofushi

Moofushi has a particular identity, which has developed over the many years that the island has been under private Italian ownership (or long lease to be more exact).

This identity is its strength and source of continuing success. The rapid expansion of the top end of the market and the continual upgrading of formerly modest resorts do, however, show up Moofushi's physical style and appearance.

The resort rooms have long been sold only through Best Tours, one of Italy's most exclusive tour operators. It is a place where celebrities, top executives and the rich can come and know they won't be bothered. It's a place to get away, to escape the pressured life and to rediscover the pleasures of simplicity. In an almost rustic setting, the regulars of Moofushi meet up year after year, as if dropping into their private club on the equator.

The atmosphere this creates is the secret of the resort. And the secret behind the secret is the longevity and attitude of the owners, management and staff. There is a togetherness and human commitment to the cause that is striking. From the owner meeting and reminiscing with guests over a pre-prandial prosecco to the pastry chef of 15 years service taking them on at volleyball, the resort does welcoming very well indeed. In several ways Moofushi acts like an extended family frequently reuniting.

During Christmas and August the children arrive on holiday whereas the rest of the year is mostly for the older members of the family. This is an all-Italian resort but not of the active type with animators. Peace and quiet is appreciated and although there is a board advertising the daily activities they are more along the lines of gentle stretching than boom boom aerobics.

Having said that, big game fishing has long been a popular activity here as the resort lies between two oceanic channels. There are regular catches of marlin, sail fish, yellow fin tuna and so on brought back, measured and photographed.

There are two guided snorkel trips to the housereef from the beach every day and these are excellent for much the same reason. The current in the channel (sometimes strong) attracts many of the big fish and has promoted coral regrowth. Each snorkel is rewarding but just in case that tires, the resort also puts on two or three free snorkel trips a week by boat.

The dive base is prominently located at the end of the main jetty, which reflects its popularity. The dive base leader has been there forever and its reputation has grown strongly over the years. For some guests, this is indeed the main purpose of their holiday.

Every guest is on a full-board package and whatever the primary motivation for coming to Moofushi, the food, if not quite up there with the very best resorts, seems always to be appreciated and lingered over. The three buffets per day can be varied with the occasional à la carte treat at the Bougainville restaurant. This specialist seafood (and Australian beef) restaurant, split between an over-water deck and a second floor balcony, offers something extra special to be enjoyed under the stars and accompanied by a fine wine.

The only thing that is disappointing about Moofushi is the room interiors. At best they can be described as simple. The beach rooms are relatively large - a second and third bed for children is not a problem - but for a resort in this high category, the style and the materials used are not what you would expect. This is even more true of the waterbungalows, which were rebuilt rather quickly after the tsunami and it is evident.

Moofushi, nonetheless, is a resort that adds up to more than the sum of its parts. As mentioned at the top, it is the atmosphere that really makes the place. It is everything together that still gives this resort a special identity.

T 666 0516 F 666 0577
E nika_htl@dhivehinet.net.mv
www.nikamaldive.com

North Ari Atoll

 20 mins

 $4

 $2.30

 $4.40

 $30

 $15

 Albatros

$75

6 x $420

PADI $550

Nika

People fall in love with Nika. They can't help themselves coming back, year after year, drawn irresistibly by its beauty and personality.

Yet, just like in human attraction, the resort won't necessarily appeal to everybody who encounters it.

Designed by an Italian and owned by an Italian, the guests were Italian for the first 20 years of the resort's life. Over the last few years other nationalities have discovered it, fallen in love with it too, but not quite made it their own. The ambience is still Italian; the look is loose white linens and cottons with open necks showing rich tans. You might say Nika today is cosmopolitan with Italian characteristics.

The unique aspect of Nika is the level of privacy you can have when you want it. Each land room is hidden in a wreath of greenery and has its own private beach, defined by a groyne on either side. The groynes, sometimes large, will disturb some more than others and they do mean you can't walk around the island, but that is the nature of a holiday here: undisturbed intimacy mixed with sociability when you wish.

A single sandy path runs in an oval around the inside of the island. It leads you through an equatorial garden of flowers and shrubs, shaded by arches of white and purple bougainvillea and the blazing red flowers of the flame tree, passing the majestic banyan tree that gives the resort its name. Grey herons nest in the banyan tree and lovebirds, along with others, delight the walker with the uncommon sound of birdsong.

The owner Mr. Balasi's love of gardening is seen again in the model fruit, vegetable and herb plot. The fresh produce finds its way onto the dining table where, famously, the quality of the ingredients is integral to Italian cuisine. And in this we have another of the reasons to fall in love with Nika.

With one restaurant only and a small number of guests, all on full board, the chef is able to prepare perfect plates for the evening meal, served at your table from an à la carte choice. With candlelight and the moonlit sights and sounds of the lagoon coming in through the open arches, it can't fail to be romantic.

Breakfast and lunch are buffets, which are also very good though the piped music of old standards might rankle a bit with some.

Evenings are generally very quiet but the daytime sees several popular excursions to local inhabited, uninhabited and desert islands. These are all very reasonably priced, which, I must say, is true of everything on the resort and very welcome. A long-time speciality of Nika is trawling for big game fish. Ibrahim, a local, is considered to be the cleverest fisherman around and many a guest comes back especially for these trips.

The dive base has been run for many years by Rainer and Robert who now completely understand the wishes of Nika's guests. They provide personal dive courses and diving trips in small groups that the clients appreciate. They appreciate not having to even wash their equipment too.

Snorkeling is excellent here and easily accessible from every room. The lagoon too is ideal: clear, sandy, not too shallow and not too big. The beach inevitably varies but with the groynes in place there is good beach at least at low tide for every room and some rooms have a permanent fine beach.

The land rooms come in two categories that are identical in size and layout but differ only in extra facilities and location. Their curved, shell-like design is still a unique delight even if a few top resorts have surpassed them in size. At 70 square metres, with a huge bathroom, wooden parquet flooring and a mix of eclectic and homely furnishing, these are rooms that still compete at the top level. One Sultan Suite with two bedrooms and bathrooms (and 110 sqm) is ideal for a family or a group of friends.

The ten new waterbungalows represent the high style of resort life. Three conical thatched roofs cover the designer bathroom, the chic lounge and the bedroom and - this being Nika - completely hide a large wooden deck for ultimate privacy. Steps take you down to the perfect lagoon and a few strokes away from great snorkeling.

Nika is still Nika, unique, beautiful, classy and private.

| 1 | 2 | 3 | 4 | 5 | 6 | 7 | 8 | 9 | 10 | | 1 | 2 | 3 | 4 | 5 | 6 | 7 | 8 | 9 | 10 |
| LOWEST | | RELATIVE PRICE | | | HIGHEST | | | | | | MOST | | | ROOM DENSITY | | | | | LEAST |

T 664 2788 F 664 5942
E info@olhuveli.com.mv
www.olhuveli.com

Images below courtesy of Olhuveli

South Male Atoll

 50 mins

 160 mins

 $5.50

 $4.25

 $4.20

1/2 $33

 $22

 Sun International

$65

6 x $372

PADI $695

Olhuveli is a modern resort with a mix of everything. It is an active place with varied facilities and entertainment, but it is also possible to enjoy a quiet holiday if you take a more distant waterbungalow.

There are two sets of waterbungalows off the island, and the more expensive the rooms the further away they are from the busy centre. Two Presidential Suites sit proudly at the tip of the jetty at one end of the island. Alongside them are the five Honeymoon Water Villas. The remainder of the oval-shaped jetty is lined with 32 Jacuzzi Water Villas. The second water-bungalow jetty extends from the middle of the island and holds the 21 Deluxe Water Villas.

The Honeymoon Villas are almost apartments, with a 'cloakroom' by the entrance and a separate sitting room. Their deck is very large and has not only a proper jacuzzi but also a steam and massage shower cubicle. The jacuzzis of the Jacuzzi Water Villas are bathtubs with nozzles but their position on the deck is excellent, especially for those on the west side. They look out to the nearby sandbank and away to distant islands. Inside, they boast marble floor tiles, blue and gold upholstery and swagged curtains, more than enough dark wood furniture and a stylish bathroom with twin beaten metal washbasins.

The Deluxe Water Villas are simpler but no less attractive for that, especially with their muslin draped four-poster beds. The deck has good privacy and is large enough for two cushioned loungers and chairs. The views are less good, though, with one side looking out to a man-made 'peninsula' and sandbank and the other side looking over to the other water-bungalow jetty. That is, except for the rooms at the tip, which have unimpeded views out to sea.

The land rooms come in two categories: 8 Luxury Beach Villas and 96 Deluxe Beach Villas. The Luxury Beach Villas are individual and private, with their own quiet area of beach. They have a large inside/outside bathroom that is very pleasant, even though the empty pergola at the end is redundant. The main drawback is their positioning near the main bar. The fun and music, usually placed outside, can go on till late into the night.

The Deluxe Beach Villas come in blocks of four, two up and two down. Three blocks (12 rooms) have an interconnecting door for families. They are the smallest rooms on the island but smartly decorated and well maintained. All of them are just a couple of steps away from the beach. For these rooms the nearer the centre of the island the better. One reason is that the island and the beach are less attractive towards the staff area end and the other reason is guests will be nearer all the activity centres. That is important in this case because most of these rooms are taken by the Italian clientele.

Around half the guests are Italian and the other half a mix of German, British and Japanese. The Italian guests come with Azemar and enjoy their own sort of holiday. Of the two swimming pools, they gather around the bigger one with a children's pool, daily aqua aerobics and a large beach. Here too is a gym, a poolroom, a karaoke lounge and the doctor's clinic.

The excursions, as usual, are particularly popular with the Italians and the nightly musical entertainment in the main bar is a regular gathering. A huge deck between the bar and the lagoon allows everyone to sit where they feel comfortable. Saturday night is Maldivian Night, which is as good a cultural night as there is on any resort. Compered in Italian and English it covers many aspects of local traditional life interspersed with dancing to the Boduberu drums.

The resort still has a new feel to it and while the landscape is still growing in, the facilities are all smart and impressive. The pool table and gym have their own rooms and so do table tennis and darts, which are next door to the floodlit tennis and badminton courts. The watersports centre is comprehensive and up-to-date. With the majority of guests on all-inclusive packages, however, they find it a bit disappointing that everything has a charge.

The lagoon is good for watersports, being large, quite shallow and sandy bottomed. At low tide it is only about knee deep but there are large channels dug into it that are always good for swimming. Snorkeling happens either side of the main jetty for about 500 metres in total. The reef is not good but the fish life is fine. There is a weekly snorkeling safari to three excellent reefs.

The spa is large and Chinese in concept but the therapists are Indonesian, Thai and Indian. It also has two rooms for hair and beauty treatments.

Olhuveli is well priced for what it has to offer and it will surely get better in the coming years.

1 2 3 4 5 6 7 8 **9** 10	1 2 3 4 5 6 7 8 **9** 10	T 662 0044 F 662 0033
LOWEST RELATIVE PRICE HIGHEST	MOST ROOM DENSITY LEAST	E info@oneandonlykanuhura.com.mv
		www.oneandonlyresorts.com

Lhaviyani Atoll

 40 mins

 $6.60

 £7.70

 $8.80

 $65

 $41

 Sun

 $81

6 x $426

PADI $700

One & Only Kanuhura

Kanuhura is indeed the one and only resort that combines such an array of spa and beauty treatments, and health and fitness activities, with an unmatched Kids' Club, fine dining and a luxurious setting.

Not a single groyne breaks up the beach and no sea walls impede the view. The west side is nonetheless preferable for its width and softness. The east side looks out to the ocean and the beach is consequently narrower and a little less fine. The southern and northern tips of the island alternate a big bulge of fine sand as the two seasons drive it from one end to the other. It's a rare island now that leaves the beach to nature's course.

The vast, empty lagoon is perfect for swimming and for watersports. The wind cuts across at an ideal angle to sail the catamarans and windsurfers up and down. There's plenty of protected water too for water-skiing, wakeboarding and kite surfing. The centre does regular catamaran excursions to nearby islands and to Kuredu for the snorkeling. A big bonus is the frequent sighting of dolphins, and occasionally pilot whales, in this tip of Llaviyani Atoll.

The downside of such a lagoon is the absence of housereef snorkeling. To compensate, the dive base runs guided trips every day to a number of good local spots, the most fascinating of which is 'The Shipyard', where two wrecks are located, one of which is partly above the waterline. Wolle, the dive base leader, describes this as the best wreck site in the country.

Though the diving set-up is excellent, it is the spa complex that takes centre stage on Kanuhura. The prominence of the large and attractive thatched building seems to set the resort's priorities. It invites you to use it on a daily basis as an integral part of your holiday.

The interior of the spa, though, doesn't quite fulfill the promise of the entrance. It has all the facilities one could wish for but the setting and the eight smallish treatment rooms are more straight-lined and formal than open-aired, soft and natural. That is not to take anything away from the very experienced masseuses.

In the same building is a very busy beauty salon, a gym and an aerobics space. In some ways these are as central to the resort concept now as the spa itself. There is a full weekly schedule of complimentary classes in everything from Pilates and Yogacise to Power Stretch, Absolute Abs and Aero Combo. One & Only Kanuhura is really into the whole family, with something for everyone to be doing.

A key policy of the owning company is being attractive to children and so it is here. An active Kids' Club runs throughout the day, while trained babysitters can care for smaller children. No other resort offers swimming lessons for children, or treasure hunts or lessons about the reef, the stars and local crafts. Understandably, the resort entertains a lot of children, during the school holidays in particular.

At these times, and others, there is an over-demand for the five Duplex Villas, which have a double bedroom with a twin bedroom interconnected. Three Beach Suites could also be used for families. The other rooms are the 70 Beach Bungalows, 18 Water Villas and two Water Suites. The Water Villas are the same as the Beach Bungalows but just a little wider. They and the Beach Suites are on the east side but the most popular rooms are those on the west side, with the advantages of sunset, a finer beach and better foliage in between the rooms.

Dining is an unadulterated pleasure here. The venues, the choice and the quality are excellent. Half-board guests (the great majority) may choose between all three restaurants: Thin Rah (the main), Olive Tree (Mediterranean) and Velhi Café (seafood, meat and live cooking). Velhi Café is on the northern tip overlooking the water, a beautifully lit, romantic place in the evening. The Olive Tree is just like the real thing, a classic and classy taverna. And the main restaurant serves up a changing menu of outstanding buffets. The breakfast buffet is perhaps the best anywhere. One small example is the choice of jams, with blood orange marmalade, quince preserve, lemon curd, two honeys and, it seemed, every veri veri berry!

Kanuhura offers something for everybody, wonderful food and tip top service. It seemed to me, however, the mix of clientele, the differences in ages, attitudes and expectations, just fail to make the place click as a single resort. Otherwise it's one of the best.

1	2	3	4	5	6	7	8	9	10
LOWEST   RELATIVE PRICE   HIGHEST

1	2	3	4	5	6	7	8	9	10
MOST   ROOM DENSITY   LEAST

T 664 8800 F 664 8855
E info@oneandonlyresorts.com.mv
www.oneandonlyresorts.com

Images below courtesy of Only & Only Reethi Rah

North Male Atoll

 50 mins

 $6

 $7

 $4.50

 $165

Reethi Rah

 $88

5 x $400

PADI $720

One & Only Reethi Rah

The luxury resort company One & Only has spent a phenomenal amount of money turning the beautiful island of Reethi Rah into their flagship property.

It has been conceived and built quite brilliantly and stocked with the world's finest food, drink and equipment (to say nothing of the staff). It will take another year or so, however, before the natural environment approaches the attractiveness of the built environment.

Three quarters of the present resort is man-made. The vast extension of the original island to create curves of new beaches with widely spaced villas, and water-bungalows extending from the 'headlands', was a staggering project and is unique in the country. Its final success requires time for nature to blossom in Maldives' unhelpful soil.

As I entered a room for the first time, I had an involuntary intake of breath. Like a private royal chapel the sense of space, height and luxury lifts your spirits and calms your mind. Extending away in front of you, under a high vaulted ceiling, the bedroom and lounge flow through to the open bathroom and on to the shower room, where, on the back wall, a four-metre mirror seems to double the space again. One moves from the 30" flat-screen surround sound home cinema and the broadband internet connection to the satin finished Egyptian cotton linens of the bed, on to the utterly romantic double bath of shaped and polished terrazzo and ends with a choice of rainforest shower or power shower on alternate sides of this exquisite rectangle.

On the land are 54 Beach Villas, six Duplex Villas (twin villas for families) and five Grand Beach Villas. On the water are 30 Water Villas and two Grand Water Villas, on eight separate jetties around the island. The first numbered rooms, particularly for the beach villas, are the best located because the vegetation in this southwest corner is well advanced and the beaches are finer too.

Built from the ground up, the opportunity to design in spectacular sightlines all around the island has been truly grasped. Combining those sightlines with grand opulence, the striking main restaurant and bar building is reminiscent of a temple. A floor to ceiling glass cube - the cold kitchen - lies at the centre. Off this are three themed seating areas utilising soaring painted pillars, carved columns, five-metre long teak tables, water features and blue glass tiles.

The bar connects to the restaurant but looks out to the free-form swimming pool. It boasts the largest collection of champagnes in the country and twenty types of bottled water. Perhaps not for the simple at heart, even the breakfast comes from a crafted à la carte menu.

One specialist restaurant is Middle Eastern with an outrageous "boho-chic" setting of carpets on the sand, giant cushions and crystal chandeliers hung from the palms. Great fun and given drive by the resort's terrific music selection - the best I have come across. The other specialist restaurant is an ultra sophisticated Japanese place, also on the water's edge, with a mother of pearl bar and tables of arresting beauty.

One & Only look after children better than anyone. The fact that there are only six family villas indicates that not so many are brought along, but those that are must have a great time here. A KidsOnly club for 2-11 year olds sees them constructively entertained all day and a ClubOne for teenagers is a loosely structured hang-out packed with good things. In the neighbourhood are the watersports centre, football pitch, tennis academy and dive centre.

The spa, run by ESPA and occupying an extensive waterfront area, is as thoroughgoing as would be expected. The mental, spiritual or just physical journey starts with a personal consultation to define a tailor-made programme of treatments and, if desired, dietary plans. The options are myriad and the staff highly trained. For a stiffer workout, the gym next door wows you with the very latest in modern equipment (Kinesis).

The built environment, as I have said, is quite wonderful. Nature is not so well served up. The housereef is not accessible for snorkeling and there is little in the lagoon to excite. The beaches do not approach Maldives' finest and the water in the cup-shaped 'bays' is not crystal clear. Cultured orchids are pretty and profuse, but the planted palms and flowers are only slowly transforming the hot, open interior. It will be a while yet before we can design nature as successfully as everything else.

| 1 | 2 | 3 | 4 | 5 | 6 | **7** | 8 | 9 | 10 | | 1 | 2 | 3 | 4 | 5 | 6 | 7 | 8 | 9 | **10** |

LOWEST   RELATIVE PRICE   HIGHEST   MOST   ROOM DENSITY   LEAST

T 662 0087 F 662 0091
Ereservations@sportingholiday.com.mv
www.palmbeachmaldives.com

 Lhaviyani Atoll

 35 mins

 $4

 $4

 $4

 inc

 inc

Palm Beach

$58

5 x $330

PADI $425

Palm Beach

On an old, once inhabited island, Palm Beach successfully maintains the line between minimal impact and full facilities.

There are no groynes or sea walls here, the wide and wonderful beaches are allowed to shift with the seasons. In the long run this is the best idea, but it does mean that, seasonally, some rooms have just a small amount of beach outside. This is particularly the case with the 20, more expensive, two-storey, Villa rooms. On the other hand, these rooms are built in the shady, palm and flower-studded end of the island, near to the main buildings and the delightful, specialist restaurant.

The opposite half of the island is more or less open to the skies and here we find the 25 Deluxe Superior rooms and 55 Deluxe rooms. The advantage of these rooms is as one moves further away from the public area everything becomes even more quiet and the beaches even more untouched. The rooms themselves are large and pleasant enough, though, like all the buildings here, rather 'blocky'. Textiles, patterned on the traditional mat designs, bring a welcome warmth. All the rooms have piped music, televisions with many satellite channels and in-house movies. The prime rooms are the four Presidential Suites.

It is in the nature of this place that everything is laid on but nothing is pushed. All watersports, apart from diving, are free for the asking. As is tennis, squash, table tennis and pool. All excursions and fishing trips are also free. The guest relations people and the tour reps quietly move through the restaurant in the evenings chatting and informing guests about what is happening at any time. It is noticeable that the resort is very well managed and that the staff are friendly and enthusiastic.

The intimate atmosphere engendered by drinks and live music in the pool bar dissipates a little as guests move into the vast restaurant. This, the main bar, the coffee shop and reception were built for a resort with many more rooms than were finally built, so it takes a full complement of amicable Italian guests to fill the places out.

All guests come on full-board basis and the food, it must be said, is faultless. An Italian bias to a continental cuisine, it is all fresh, varied and sure to satisfy. The salads and deserts are unusually good, as is the sizzling meat and fish grill outside. Although almost everyone is on full board, there is a temptation at some point to check out the small, classy à la carte restaurant, beautifully sited beside the beach, beneath the palms.

Italians are a little over half the population here and the ambience is molded by them. The large minority is made up of Germans, French, Swiss and Japanese, who also seem to thoroughly enjoy what the resort has to offer. Essentially what it offers is good food, large rooms, lots of facilities and a varied, pretty island.

1 2 3 4 **5** 6 7 8 9 10   1 2 3 **4** 5 6 7 8 9 10
LOWEST   RELATIVE PRICE   HIGHEST   MOST   ROOM DENSITY   LEAST

T 664 0011 F 664 0022
E info@paradise-island.com.mv
www.villahotels.com

North Male Atoll

20 mins

$3.85

$3.30

$3.85

1/2 $33

$30

Delphis

$70

5 x $325

PADI $595

Paradise Island

Paradise Island is a popular resort. It's just fifteen minutes from the airport, it's very friendly and there are loads of things to do.

Add sunshine and you've got the makings of an enjoyable holiday. It is a long way, though, from the small, natural islands with beach and reef that first come to mind when one thinks of Maldives.

The island has been redrawn and remade by man. To protect the extended land from erosion a substantial wall of coral rubble and sand was built in the lagoon around half the island. It is unsightly and blocks the views of a 100 rooms (241-341), though half of these (241-286) are some 200 metres away and, facing west, they enjoy the afternoon sun.

With 260 rooms in all, there are plenty with clear views (particularly 174-240). Of the total, 220 are Beach Bungalows and 40 are Waterbungalows. Half the Waterbungalows face north and half face south. They are spacious, well-appointed rooms in great demand. Steps drop down to the lagoon, which is fine for swimming (though it gets very shallow at low tide) and there are little bits of snorkeling here and there.

The Beach Bungalows are similar in size and decor (slightly less 'grand'), only they step out to beach rather than water. A beach that is not uniformly good. This is due to the fact that it is man-made and needs to be re-covered at intervals with new soft sand. A line of trees gives shade to the rooms and between it and the beach is a flat, open area with space to maneuver the lounger to follow the sun. Even this is not always the case, so some negotiation to change rooms may be desired.

One of the resort's strong points is certainly the management and staff. The long-time general manager, Shujau, is a calm and very capable guy who is himself responsible for several guests returning here for their holidays again and again. The same would be true of a number of waiters and room boys for this is one of the keys to Paradise Island's success. A rapport is often struck up with the staff and this sets an easygoing atmosphere that encourages friendliness between the guests.

Your waiter at breakfast will detail the list of up-coming excursions and special events, and take your booking after you've chewed it over. The options are many and varied. Fishing comes in four varieties: early morning, sunset with a group, trawling for tuna and big game fishing. Being close to Male and the airport gives you the option not only of shopping and sightseeing in the capital but also of photo flights and a trip on a mini-submarine.

The food in the main restaurant is fairly good but it's much better in the other outlets, so be prepared for a bit of an overspend here. A quiet seafood restaurant faces out to the open ocean and a Japanese restaurant looks authentic, but the star is an Italian restaurant at the end of the arrival jetty. This has such a reputation that guests motor in from Male and nearby five-star resorts.

Sports give you more options still, with floodlit tennis and indoor squash and badminton (non a/c). The watersports centre has all the usual kit in very good condition, plus parasailing and kite surfing. And there's a fine little spa on the quiet northern tip of the resort. As is now usual, each pavilion has twin treatment tables so couples can enjoy the pleasure together.

The swimming pool is small for a big resort but the decking integrates smoothly with the main bar and the whole works well, particularly in the evenings as the fun fills up and spills out of the bar. A large number of nationalities make up the guests, with many East Asians in particular, but the pub is mostly the domain of the Europeans, particularly the British and Germans.

There is some good diving around although, as the longest established and busiest resort region, the sites are well used. There is almost no snorkeling on the resort unfortunately, just a patch beside the arrival jetty, but there are daily snorkel trips organised.

1	2	**3**	4	5	6	7	8	9	10
LOWEST		RELATIVE PRICE			HIGHEST				

1	2	3	4	5	6	7	8	9	10
MOST			ROOM DENSITY				LEAST		

T 668 0828 F 668 0823
E info@ranvelivillage.com
www.ranvelivillage.com

South Ari Atoll

 25 mins

 105 mins

 $3.65

 $3.30

 $4.40

1/2 $33

 $22

 Ranveli

 $52

10 x $420

PADI $585

Ranveli

Through ill luck of one sort and another Ranveli has fallen on hard times. A once thriving all-Italian club resort is now struggling to get back to its former occupancy and good looks.

The Italian holiday company went bankrupt, other financial issues made matters worse and a new Maldivian management took over a bad situation. Maintenance all around has suffered and sadly the beach, which was never extensive, has continued to erode.

The good news is another resort is now open to every nationality (amongst the biggest spread of nationalities of any resort) and at a very good price. New developments are steadily taking place and a positive local management should be able to reestablish its reputation.

The layout of the resort is very simple. Two rows of two-storey rooms run down the middle of the thin island. At one end is the service area; at the other is a tongue of sand. The straight interior path is prettily dressed with flowers, arches of bougainvillea and shrubs. One enters the rooms from here and glass sliding doors open out to the other side, which for a lucky few is the beach but for many is only space enough for a sunlounger before the water's edge or a supporting wall.

The main, indeed the only, beach is a bulge of sand on the south side, which runs into a tongue of sand drifting into the lagoon. It's all lovely and fine underfoot but only Italian guests really enjoy being all together on the beach every day. And this is no longer an Italian resort, although remnants do linger. The chefs still turn out Italian dishes and man a live pasta station twice a day.

The biggest reminder is the nineteenth-century style pier pavilion that stretches out over the water. Its large rooms and corridors are decorated with painted glass panels, pastel floral cutouts, arched fanlights and leaded chandeliers. Where once pre-prandial drinks, music and group dancing sessions filled out the building, extending after dinner to a nightly cabaret, the place now has the echo of an old seaside pavilion out of season. But this is Maldives and it might already have found a new life and purpose.

The rooms themselves are in very good order. Decorated in ivory and tans with simple, quality fixtures and fittings they look classy and feel good. The bathrooms have a large bath, a good shower and a marble basin top. There's also a side area for the wardrobe, dressing table, mirror and minibar.

Some people prefer upstairs rooms for their extra privacy and views, but most people don't and so there are probably too many rooms for the island's size.

This area of South Ari Atoll has many well-loved dive sites, which is a big plus for potential divers, and for snorkelers the reef drop-off is as close as any resort in the country (the neighbours Vilamendhoo and Lily Beach have similar distances). The quality of the snorkeling is OK but coral regrowth has been slow, perhaps due to the vertical wall and the prevailing fast-moving current.

Ranveli then is a resort in the process of getting back to its best, of redefining itself for future success.

1	2	3	4	**5**	6	7	8	9	10

LOWEST   RELATIVE PRICE   HIGHEST

1	2	3	4	5	6	**7**	8	9	10

MOST   ROOM DENSITY   LEAST

T 660 2626   F 660 2727
E info@reethibeach.com.mv
www.reethibeach.com

Baa Atoll

 35 mins

 $3.70

 $3.30

 $3.90

 $39

 $25

Sea Explorer

 $60

6 x $312

 PADI $600

Reethi Beach

Where once Reethi Beach was a fine island but an ordinary resort, today it is a superb all-round resort, outstanding value for money and still a great island.

A really good man at the top turned the feel of the place around. The staff of men and women, Maldivian and European, convey a sense of happiness and willingness that enthuses the guests.

The look too has been renovated to great effect. A modern comfortable chic, echoing the style of its neighbour Soneva Fushi, gives a tingle of privilege. Tasteful wooden furniture backs a vitalizing colour scheme taken from the flower of a native tree: yellow on the bow turning to orange with a deep red when on the floor.

The natural look and feel blend perfectly with the nature of the island. This is one of the resort islands most blessed by nature and, as reflected in the Green Award granted by Kuoni, Reethi Beach is committed to keeping it as undisturbed as possible.

Not only have the four thousand plus trees been protected and never sprayed but also the beach still remains without a single groyne or wall. Furthermore, there hasn't been any pumping of sand onto the beach, so the quality remains perfect and the reef hasn't suffered from run-off.

There is an excellent beach all the way down the west side, where the Reethi Villas are, and an even wider bulge of fine sand at the southern end, where the Deluxe Villas are. At the other end is a smaller bulge behind the semi-circle of waterbungalows. This is an uncommon bonus for waterbungalow guests, particularly as there are plenty of thatched umbrellas and a hut bar open all day.

On the other hand it is fortunate the beach is nearby as only the rooms at the ends of the semi-circle catch the sun, the others face north. The balconies are a bit small and there are no steps down to the water (they are on the walkway) but the view is splendid - spotless and serene.

Inside, the waterbungalows are more spacious than most and nicely put together. On the parquet style floor stands a large double bed and a long sofa that could double as another bed. There is a CD player as well as satellite television, a kettle for tea and coffee, a safe, minibar and hairdryer.

The island rooms are, in my opinion, slightly better as they are equally well furnished, they all have clear views to the sea and are just a few steps from a fine beach and good snorkeling. Aside from the larger beach, the Deluxe Villas have extra space plus a bathtub inside and a swing joli outside.

Reethi Beach is what you might call quietly active. The general air is tranquil and unhurried but there are far more options for action here than on most resorts. Two tennis courts abut the indoor sports complex that has two squash courts, two badminton courts and a gym. Staff members give inexpensive lessons and are available to play against you. The complex opens out to a small swimming pool with loungers and umbrellas. In a room off the main bar you can continue with table tennis and table football and round by the beach bar you can join in the daily beach volleyball game.

The watersports centre, with its prominent position on the beach, is active and very well stocked. This is one of the few places you can try out kite surfing, for example. Sailing or windsurfing trips can have one of several nearby sandbanks and desert islands as a destination. The resort looks after four desert islands that are also used for one-couple-only Robinson Crusoe picnics.

The Coconut Spa is nothing much to look at but the Balinese therapists are superb and the prices, as everywhere here, are very reasonable.

The cuisine in all the outlets is remarkably good, which is especially unusual as up to 50% of the guests here are on all-inclusive deals. The main restaurant offers such variety that the lunch buffet is different every day for a fortnight. Having said that, it is the specialist restaurants that show the real flair and enjoyment of the chefs. Argentina Night at the grill and any night at the over-water Moodhu Restaurant are holiday highlights.

Another highlight for many will be the diving. Around a third of the Brits, Germans, Swiss and Austrians who come here go diving and that's as high as anywhere. With only a few inactive resorts in the atoll the many sites are still fresh and relatively unvisited. Angelo's dive team run a great centre organising up to four dives a day. Many of the sites (including the housereef) are illustrated in their terrific souvenir logbook.

1	2	3	4	**5**	6	7	8	9	10
LOWEST		RELATIVE PRICE			HIGHEST				

1	2	3	**4**	5	6	7	8	9	10
MOST			ROOM DENSITY			LEAST			

T 664 1994   F 664 0052
E info@rihiveli-maldives.com
www.rihiveli-maldives.com

South Male Atoll

 50 mins

 $3

 $3.50

 $2.50

 inc

 inc

 Eurodivers

 $53

5 x $245

PADI $522

Rihiveli

Rihiveli is a special resort with a distinctive French ambience. It is one of the few places that remain simple, open, rustic and combine this with excellent facilities and genuine service.

A narrow sandy path leads from the top of the jetty right through the middle of the island. The rooms and beach are on either side. There are no concrete paths, no swimming pool, no a/c. It is a place where well-off French (80%) come to switch off hectic Europe and live a simpler life for a while.

The resort is something of a sophisticated club where most of the facilities and activities are included, where people make acquaintances around the mixed dinner tables and enjoy evenings of light entertainment together, organised by the big, cheerful, informal Baba.

Everyone is on full board and the meals, in a thatched over-water restaurant, are as good as you would expect, with particularly impressive salads and fruits. For lunch there is always the option of a barbecue on the neighbouring desert island, to which you wade out, canoe or sail.

There are in fact two desert islands in the lagoon for the guests' pleasure. The second is an even more secluded 'bird island'. To reach them, or just for recreation, all the watersports are free of charge. Lessons too are freely given by a notably friendly staff. Waterskiing happens twice a day from a pontoon in the deeper water.

The lagoon is too big and shallow to be ideal but natural swimming pools have been created off both sides of the island. The reef is inaccessible from the beach but two free snorkel trips a day are included. Indeed all the excursions are included in the price of your holiday.

The most popular excursion, unsurprisingly, is the 'bivouac', where two to four people spend a full day cruising around the atoll to the south, visiting inhabited and uninhabited islands and then sleeping on deck under the stars. The other excursions are of the usual variety though they do also offer serious big game fishing (for which you pay serious money).

The beach that looks into the lagoon, the sunset side, is finer than the other side, which is augmented by pumped sand and has a low lagoon wall. But the view to the open sea takes in the two beautiful islets. On such a narrow island, there is little to choose in terms of location, especially since every room has its own private setting of a beach and view to water.

Each of the 24 'L' shaped cottages contains two rooms, featuring a compact modern bathroom, a small but attractive bedroom and a curved verandah with low chairs and loungers. On a couple of nearby trees hangs your hammock. Rustic elegance is the style and philosophy, right down to the fan but no a/c and hot water in the shower but not the basin.

Echoes of the South Pacific are evident in the beautifully designed bar and games building, with its high thatched roof that slopes sharply down and reaches low to the ground around its open sides. Right in the middle of the island (and next to the similarly designed new boutique) this place becomes the focus around sunset when guests gather to watch the daily spectacle accompanied by the strains of Beethoven and Mozart. After dinner the place fills up again for fun, games and camaraderie.

The final key to Rihiveli is the attitude of the staff. It is always friendly and informal yet helpful and efficient too. The staff create an inclusive, family atmosphere. Tellingly, a considerable number of them, both Maldivian and European, have been with the resort for many, many years. Similarly, a good number of Rihiveli guests have been coming back for many, many years.

| 1 | 2 | 3 | 4 | 5 | **6** | 7 | 8 | 9 | 10 |
LOWEST   RELATIVE PRICE   HIGHEST

| 1 | 2 | 3 | 4 | 5 | **6** | 7 | 8 | 9 | 10 |
MOST   ROOM DENSITY   LEAST

T 660 0088   F 660 0099
E info@royal-island.com
www.royal-island.com

Baa Atoll

 30 mins

$4.95

$4.70

$5.50

$70

$33

Delphis

$71

5 x $330

PADI $595

Royal Island

Royal Island is the leading property of the Villa family of resorts - the others being Sun, Fun, Paradise and Holiday.

It is built along the same straight, solid lines but uses more luxurious materials - lots of dark wood and rich textiles - and offers an even higher quality of facilities. It's a pretty island inside but the beach and snorkeling are disappointing for a top class resort.

Two Presidential Suites take over the sunset and sunrise tips of the island, while the other 148 identical rooms stretch around the perimeter between them (of these ten are interconnecting family rooms). Though they are close to each other, decent foliage and a solid build mean neighbours are unheard and usually unseen. These are not large rooms but they are expensively furnished. Dark wooden furniture with carved decoration, wood paneled walls, heavy marble table tops and thick covers and drapes in gold and maroons give them a distinctly aristocratic look and feel.

The large, two-bedroomed Presidential Suites are more of the same, and some - an expensive confection of 'chandelier luxury', well suited to the Russian and Arab markets. The spacious verandah and swimming pool are certainly pleasant and lead out through a gap in the enclosing tree line to what amounts to a private beach and lagoon. The sunrise suite enjoys the best beach on the island but serious erosion has destroyed the beach on the sunset side. (A seawall is planned to deal with this.)

A good 20 rooms on this northwest corner (211 to 235) are similarly without a beach and are consequently the very last to be given out. The rest of the island enjoys some degree of beach, although it is often rather narrow and, with tree cover, it is not always easy to position the sunlounger to catch the rays. Being at least partly man-made (i.e. pumped from the lagoon) the sand is also not of the finest.

The quality of the build, furnishings and facilities are the real strong points of this resort. The free-form swimming pool with its bar and decking is an attractive focal point for much of the day, surrounded on one side by the beach and on the other side by the main bar and lounge. A separate

Fun Pub has been built for those crazy karaoke and disco nights, leaving this bar undisturbed for long social evenings.

Racquet sports fans will be delighted with this place. The pair of floodlit tennis courts, the squash court and the indoor badminton court are all first class facilities. The gym, too, can't be bettered. And the watersports centre has all the kit, from canoe to wakeboard and kite surfing.

The best facility of all, though, is the spa. Built by a team of Indonesian craftsmen, with lots of bamboo, rope and thatch, it is a delightful retreat within the retreat. Green plants and flowers abound, water trickles and tinkles off walls and fountains. The only way to improve the atmosphere is to take one of the massages - then sit back with a cup of green tea. The six pavilions each have a pair of treatment tables, which couples seem to thoroughly enjoy. A few other rooms are devoted to ayurveda, with dedicated Indian practitioners. With a long menu of treatments, whether you wish to deal with a long-term condition or just enjoy a romantic massage for two, this is a professional and charming set-up.

The à la carte restaurant enjoys a pleasant position by the water's edge, on the far side of the island from the main buildings. Specialising in barbecues and lobster meals, it's a potentially romantic getaway for the occasional evening meal. The food in the main restaurant is the usual mix of buffets, and uninspired for this class of resort.

Diving in the region is mostly about thilas, the channels being too wide for the strong currents that attract the sharks and pelagics. Schooling fish are in abundance and there are a couple of Manta points, offering an excellent chance of sightings from May through to November. The dive school is well set up for the beginner and the average diver.

Sadly, much of the housereef was reconstructed around the time the resort was built. It is not used for diving and is not in good shape for snorkeling. Both the resort and watersports centre do snorkeling trips to nearby reefs.

| 1 | 2 | 3 | 4 | 5 | 6 | 7 | 8 | 9 | **10** | | 1 | 2 | 3 | 4 | 5 | 6 | 7 | 8 | 9 | **10** |

LOWEST   RELATIVE PRICE   HIGHEST   MOST   ROOM DENSITY   LEAST

T 660 0304 F 660 0374
E reservations-fushi@sonevaresorts.com
www.sixsenses.com

Images above courtesy of Soneva Fushi

Baa Atoll

30 mins

$5

$4

$8

$150

Soleni

$81

7 x $539

PADI Scuba $525

Soneva Fushi

I have always considered Soneva Fushi to be the best resort in the country. But that seems a modest claim now that it has been voted 'The Best of the Best' by Condé Nast Traveller's readers.

This resort doesn't just have character it has charisma. It creates idyllic holidays underpinned by a green conscience and a holistic philosophy. The remarkable thing is it keeps getting better.

The story of its success begins before guests arrive on the island. Formalities are completed and preferences taken (for films, music, amenities and so on) in the private lounge of the seaplane company. On the boat hop from the seaplane platform to the island your shoes are requested and placed in a cotton bag. 'No news no shoes' is more than a slogan here. There isn't a check-in or even a reception on Soneva Fushi. Guests are greeted by their guest relations officer or butler (identities having been forwarded) and taken directly to their rooms, where the requested music is already playing and the DVD is on the table.

Beside the chilled sparkling Chardonnay (labeled "pour Soneva Fushi") lies a folder detailing everything there is to do and see, eat and drink on and off the island. There is also a separate folder with the full list of 400 wines and yet another folder picturing and naming the island's flora and fauna. A call to your guest relations officer or butler - called Mr. or Ms. Friday here - is all that is required to sort out any request or whim.

You may snorkel with the resident biologist to better see and appreciate the life on the housereef, which is always close by and remains one of the best. The same person leads nature walks through the island, along the lily-lined paths under the thick canopy of mature palms. This is the second largest and one of the loveliest resort islands. You might also visit the site where turtles lay their eggs on the beach. The beach itself is, yes, one of the best of all resort islands. There are no groynes and no walls, yet it runs fine and soft all the way around with just one corner showing signs of erosion.

There seems to be an endless array of good things to do - how about some stargazing, an open-air classic movie with popcorn, or cocktails and canapes on a sandbank for guests and staff? - but it all comes together as a piece because of the underlying concept of enriching experiences in a sustainable environment.

The vegetable and herb garden is organic (marigolds do a great job on the caterpillars) and the al fresco lunch is just a revelation of flavours you didn't know existed in salads. The organic fruit garden is the only one in the country. Sampling the expertly cut fruit is made the more enjoyable with a glass of champagne in hand and gazing out over the canopy from the lofty wooden deck.

It is not all about healthy eating, though: the fine dining restaurant does excellent steaks, and the wood-fired pizzas and the 40-odd homemade ice creams are to die for.

In a similar fashion the spa offers good old spine-tingling, relaxing massages but it also has an ayurvedic doctor and a professional acupuncturist. It also organises week-long retreats led by masters of reiki, meditation, pilates and personal growth.

Everywhere the architecture follows nature's precedent. The materials are warm, tactile and unrefined. There are no straight lines - anywhere: even the knives and forks, the chairs, the glasses and the pencils are irregular. There are a plethora of room sizes and styles that need to be studied before settling on one. But all of them share a natural eclecticism and seem to have grown organically, sprouting walkways, pools, balconies, footbridges, pavilions and daybeds. It is not all rustic, of course, it is chic too and all the luxuries are present, discreetly.

As with anyone who is charismatic, you want to get more and more of them. Soneva Fushi's latest innovation makes it easier for repeat guests to do just that. They can leave their holiday paraphernalia in secure air-conditioned stores ready for their return, free of charge. It just gets better and better.

T 664 0304 F 664 0305
E reservations-gili@sonevaresorts.com
www.sixsenses.com

1	2	3	4	5	6	7	8	9	10
LOWEST		RELATIVE PRICE			HIGHEST				

1	2	3	4	5	6	7	8	9	10
MOST			ROOM DENSITY				LEAST		

All images courtesy of Soneva Gili

North Male Atoll

  20 mins

   $5

   $4

   $8

1/2 $220

  $55

Ocean Paradise

  $82

5 x $385

PADI Scuba $435

Soneva Gili

For putting your mind at ease and raising your spirits there is no resort in Maldives, and few in the world I would guess, better than Soneva Gili.

Many other resorts are superior in some key aspects of a Maldives holiday, but the lack of distractions, visually and mentally, combined with mould-breaking design and fine cuisine make this place something like a sanctuary for the senses.

In startling contrast to the stolid rectangles of most rooms, Soneva Gili's waterbungalows are a series of rooms, decks, landings and rooftops that seem to emerge from each other. Some spaces are under thatch, some under open sky, some open to the water below and some can be enclosed for air-conditioning. The wooden boards and pillars come unadorned, the thatch is not concealed, the wooden furniture is handmade, the cotton covers are in single earthy or sunny colours. At the same time, every luxury of an exclusive resort is incorporated. This is rustic chic and it's a revelation.

The 29 Soneva Gili Villa Suites line three jetties. The eight Soneva Gili Residences anchored at the end of the jetties are a little bigger and have better views. The seven Soneva Gili Crusoe Residences are the same as the latter except they are cut adrift in the lagoon and enjoy completely clear views to the horizon. There is also a Soneva Gili Private Reserve, which has five separate buildings and is six times the size of the Residences. It would come alive with two full families (there's a terrific waterslide).

Nearly all the residences and a few of the villa suites have uninterrupted sightlines out to the horizon, filled only with shades of blue and turquoise (and the white of drifting clouds). The rumbles of the ocean, the breaking waves on the reef and the ripples around the room are sounds that reach deep inside you. A soundtrack on the entertainment system includes whale calls and birdsong. Transporting and meditational stuff but even with a driving rock number playing, the whole place is so friendly and personal you feel you really should be naked.

From here it's just a metaphorical step to the overwater spa. As expected it is delightful, serene and serious. Each guest is consulted on wishes and advised on therapies, and an Indian ayurvedic doctor is present to diagnose and work on specific conditions. The complex includes a gym and a relaxation room on the first floor that share the same view as the treatment room balconies - empty all the way to Australia. Two standout therapies are The Soul of Six Senses, which has two therapists "synergistically performing a facial and body massage", and the Massage Workshop, which involves two or four sessions where you learn to massage your partner.

There are no straight lines on the island. The buildings are rounded and have stucco-style finishes; nature's materials are used and left unrefined. It never feels pretentious; Soneva Gili only works hard at imitating nature, right down to the details (the mugs are dimpled, the saucers scalloped). It all helps to lift your mind out of the straight (and narrow).

The main restaurant serves breakfast and dinner, either under thatch or on the adjacent beach. Fine dining à la carte is complimented by one Mediterranean evening and one Asian Spices buffet displayed in the overwater bar. The same bar offers personal stir-fry lunches of ingredients chosen by the guests, arranged as a presentation plate and served at the table. Healthy food and fresh salads and vegetables from the resort's own garden are prominent. A range of fine wines is available from the wine cellar.

Little touches of playfulness are welcoming, such as the two mattresses lying under thatch in the middle of the pool, and the hammock strung between branches in the lagoon.

The beach in front of the pool is wide and faces directly to the sunset but it is not the softest and finest around, nor is the island vegetation as tall and thick as many. Guests canoe to a new islet to start their snorkel but the extent and the quality is not great. Nor is there a really good uninhabited island or particularly charming fishermen's island nearby. Other resorts have better natural advantages in these areas. But no other resort releases you so successfully from the hard-edged urban life we come from.

A couple I overheard booking an excursion stared at each other and then started laughing. They had both completely forgotten what day or date it was.

| 1 | 2 | 3 | 4 | 5 | 6 | 7 | 8 | 9 | 10 | | 1 | 2 | 3 | 4 | 5 | 6 | 7 | 8 | 9 | 10 |

LOWEST RELATIVE PRICE HIGHEST   MOST ROOM DENSITY LEAST

T 664 1949 F 664 1910
E siv@dhivehinet.net.mv
www.summerislandvillage.com

North Male Atoll

 10 mins

 60 mins

 90 mins

 inc

 inc

 inc

$38

$15

Diverland

$56

6 x $324

PADI $483

Summer Island

The most reasonably priced all-inclusive resort in the country, Summer Island is also one of the most relaxed and unpretentious.

It is a resort that is comfortable with what it is and what it offers: long, slow days in the sun, interspersed with snorkeling trips or diving, and long, convivial nights in the bar.

In a large lagoon on the western edge of the atoll, the housereef is too distant and, outside, too rough for snorkeling. So the resort puts on four hour-long snorkel trips every day. The first two are free and additional ones are just $3 each.

This was once a solidly German dive island. It is now three quarters German and a quarter British and although being all-inclusive has reduced the numbers, diving still plays a large part in the island's identity. For newcomers to the sport, the lagoon, with a gradual slope and sandy bottom, is ideal for learning.

The same lagoon is perfect for watersports too and this is one of the more active centres. The thatched hut sits at the end of the jetty at the top of the path down the island. With its eye-catching display of equipment, laminated pictures and special offers, sooner or later you are likely to take up on something. It might be a banana boat ride or wakeboard initiation, a parasailing high or a full-moon catamaran trip.

The 92 Standard Rooms are fairly tightly spaced around the three sides of the island. They are very simple, with a/c but not even a telephone. Each of the rooms is white and clean, has a third bed, a weak shower and a decent verandah with chairs, deck-chairs and sunloungers. They are all close to the shore with views out to sea and are likely to have a good beach too.

After judicious pumping to fill in the gaps from erosion most of the rooms are now well catered for. One side of the triangle, facing out to the open sea, has a wall running its length. Just 12 of the standard rooms are on this side (the last numbered) as well as the 16 Waterbungalows.

In a line of blocks of four, the Waterbungalows are large, solid and square. They are similar to the ones on Embudu Village, even down to the plate of glass in the wooden floors. As the premium rooms, they have a telephone, hairdryer, stocked minibar and satellite tv. The uninterrupted views to the horizon are great but the deck is way too small, you can see all your neighbours and there are no steps down to the water.

A few steps from the end of the short jetty takes Waterbungalow guests to their own numbered thatched umbrella and loungers, on a good little stretch of sand at the tip of the island. The heart of the island is not an out-of-bounds staff area but is attractively worked with palms and flowers and even a little stream and rockery. Birdsong decorates the silence, both from wild birds and the almost too successfully breeding caged birds.

In a quiet spot without rooms the Serena Spa juts out over a hidden beach into the lagoon. Staffed by two young women from Kerala it has a small but varied menu of treatments, from facials and bodyworks to ayurvedic massages and specials such as a 'divers recovery' and a 'sun lovers package'.

The restaurant serves three buffets a day and the coffee shop gives out hot drinks and sandwiches at teatime. A few paces away is the large bar, equally dark under its low thatch and equally easygoing, with sand on the floor. A disco happens every week and some light live music every other week, so this isn't a hotbed of live action but people do seem to find plenty to keep them up till late most nights.

Although everybody is on an all-inclusive package you still have to sign straight away for everything you drink. This irritant is smoothed by the attitude of the staff, which is everywhere eager and helpful. Indeed, this is one of the keys to the place. The relationship with the staff seems to make things more a matter of friendship than 'service'. And, similarly, the management is not remote but very happy to consider any suggestions and ideas.

In short, this is an economical all-inclusive that knows it's an economical all-inclusive and does the job extremely well.

| 1 | 2 | 3 | 4 | **5** | 6 | 7 | 8 | 9 | 10 | | 1 | 2 | 3 | 4 | 5 | 6 | **7** | 8 | 9 | 10 |

LOWEST   RELATIVE PRICE   HIGHEST   MOST   ROOM DENSITY   LEAST

T 668 0088 F 668 0099
E info@sun-island.com.mv
www.villahotels.com

South Ari Atoll

 35 mins

150 mins

$3.75

$3.50

$4.50

$53

$30

Little Mermaid

$62

5 x $276

PADI $682

Sun Island

Sun Island is a winner, in many ways. It represents perhaps the best value for money in the country.

Having said that, it depends entirely on what values you are looking for in a Maldives island holiday. This place is the opposite of the small island 'settle back and relax' concept. It's big and it's busy. But it still delivers the simple things that make a great holiday.

At 350 rooms this is the largest resort in the country by some way. And yet it is a big and very green island with a full circuit of beach and a long list of activities, so you don't see a lot of your fellow guests except at mealtimes and in the evenings.

Waterbungalows account for 72 of the rooms (of which four are over-the-top Presidential Suites). These, as usual, are the premium priced rooms and the interiors are designed to express this. Wood floors and wall panels, a recessed ceiling with cornicing, copper, gold and peach striped textiles, work together to give an aristocratic look and feel. A sizeable sundeck is half stone tiles and half weathered wooden boards, with sunloungers and sun chairs. Steps lead down to the lagoon.

Half the bungalows face the rising sun and half face the setting sun. Unless you are an early riser, make sure you get a sunset room. None of the rooms have much in the way of snorkeling, however, as the lagoon is uniformly shallow (one to two metres) and without coral. This makes it ideal for pottering about and swimming, of course.

All but 60 of the island rooms are designated Super Deluxe, the rest merely Deluxe. They are all semi-detached and have a good-sized verandah. Inside they are spacious, clean and tidy. 'Extras' would be a hairdryer, safe, large mirrors and satellite tv with internet access. The differences between the categories are not critical: the Deluxes are a tiny bit smaller and don't have a bathtub or bidet. They are, however, on the southwest side of the island while the best rooms are those on the east side.

At this end of the island it is quieter. You are away from the passing traffic - people walking, cycling and in vans (you call the van for free and hire the bikes). Behind the rooms are the resort's plantation and an area of natural vegetation that was deliberately left untouched during construction. Also at this end of the island is a fine bulge of sand, with the watersports centre and a beach bar in just the right spot. Rooms 211 - 248 are here and face north but a good area of open sand allows you to spin the sunlounger around to catch the rays. Rooms 249 - 288 face the sun looking south.

An area of snorkeling is available from off the deck of the Italian restaurant at the end of the arrival jetty. It doesn't look too rewarding but the fish life is surprisingly good, with sightings of rays, turtles, Napoleon wrasses, barracudas and sharks. The dive centre is encouraging and supportive of learner divers and this is a good place to start, with a clear shallow lagoon for the lessons and some world-class dive sites within an hour's boat trip. The Dhigurah Channel and Kudarah Thila to the northeast are world-renowned dive spots.

The watersports centre has the whole gamut of equipment, both motor-powered and wind-powered, all in excellent condition. This is just typical of the island (and Villa resorts in general). You will also find an excellent gym, quality floodlit tennis courts, indoor squash and badminton courts and perfect snooker tables. A $5 a day deal (minimum seven days) will cover these facilities and more, as will the all-inclusive holiday. This is recommended because the individual hire charges are not insignificant (there's even a charge to play darts). And if you are not all-inclusive you will need to pay $10 a day for the satellite tv channels.

Alongside the usual island visits, there is an early morning dolphin trip and three types of fishing - big game, sunrise line trawling and sunset. Most people do the sunset line-over-the-side fishing and the resort then cooks up the catch for an excellent barbecue that same evening. This is one of the times when people break the ice and friendships are made.

Sun Island is unquestionably a friendly place. The staff/guest relations are warm and easygoing, and the vibe around the swimming pool and in the restaurants and bars is very good, particularly in the large main bar in the evening, spilling out as it does on to beachside decking. Quiet times can be had in the golf bar (the course now sadly overgrown), private dinners and strolling around the shopping arcade. There's even a video games parlour. And a large new spa with twin treatment tables in each pavilion. It's no wonder that people leave Sun Island wondering where the time went.

1	2	3	4	5	6	**7**	8	9	10

LOWEST RELATIVE PRICE HIGHEST

1	**2**	3	4	5	6	7	8	9	10

MOST ROOM DENSITY LEAST

T 664 1948 F 664 3884
E resv@tajcoral.com.mv
www.tajhotels.com

North Male Atoll

45 mins

$6
$4
$5
$55
$45
Blue In
$70
5 x $330
PADI $664

Taj Coral Reef

This neat, compact resort is run by the Taj group, India's leading luxury hotel management company.

Attentive service, a smart setting and good food are its strengths. On the whole it is a quiet, calm retreat that is not formal but does have an air of respectability.

The management is out front and interactive, perfectly turned out and always trying to keep their guests happy. On hand at the evening entertainment, encouraging guests to join in their cricket, football or tennis games, or just listening carefully to requests, the Taj's hundred-year experience in the hospitality business is affirmed every day.

The resort is neither a very active place nor a completely quiet one. The excursion list is short and ordinary (Male excursion, Kuda Bandos picnic, night fishing and island hopping, plus a possible photo flight and whale submarine), but a sandbank some way off is used for couples to taste a desert island experience (with a bottle of champagne, of course).

The once-a-week disco on the beach is the single 'big night out' and three other nights have short, light entertainments. Otherwise the nights are for quiet drinks on the big bar deck overlooking the lagoon or reading and chatting outside the rooms.

Although not greatly used, the resort does have a gym, a full-sized snooker table and a small swimming pool. On one side of the pool is the spa, run by the famous Balinese company Mandara. The therapists are very good, the menu short and sweet, but the rooms are small and enclosed.

Strung along the slowly curving base of this rounded triangular island are the 36 Lagoon Villas. Constructed in pairs, their entrance is from the land but their balcony and views are over water (past the lagoon walls). One deck set back is large and private but the deck at the water's edge is very small and visible to all its neighbours. A few wooden steps take you down to a sandy lagoon with good coral outcrops. The first two villas look east and are very close to the snorkeling zone, the last four villas have the sunset every day and the remaining villas look northwards but do get sun on their decks.

The 30 Beach Villas are a little smaller than the Lagoon Villas but equally solidly built and equipped with satellite television and in-house movies, hairdryer, safe, minibar and tea/coffee facilities. The rooms, again in pairs, reach around the rounded tip of the triangle and, in doing so, have very different experiences of beach during the year.

From August to January the effect of the south-west wind and prevailing current pushes the sand into a very fine beach beside the main jetty and outside the restaurant, grill and first few rooms. It makes for a great focal point to the resort and its activities but at the expense of a beach in front of the remaining rooms. From February to March the beach moves back to give these rooms a fine beach, but this reduces the beach of the first few rooms and resort frontage to a rump of sand.

Snorkeling is very good on Taj Coral Reef. The housereef is accessible all around, although with the area outside the Lagoon Villas off-bounds for half the year due to strong currents, the really good snorkeling area is not very extensive. Having said that, a housereef wreck three minutes from the beach is a big bonus. Surprisingly there are no snorkeling trips on the excursion list.

Diving is well established here and, set in the middle of the western side of the atoll, many varied dive sites are within easy reach by dhoni.

The three main nationalities enjoying their holiday here are Italian, Japanese and British. Other guests come from India, France, Korea and China. Expectation of high standards is a common denominator of these guests and perhaps nowhere is this expectation more visibly met than in the restaurant.

The high thatched roof, open sides and views out to the beach or inside to the swimming pool make for a setting worthy of the cuisine. As you would expect, Indian curries are a speciality of the house. A renowned Japanese chef resides for a month a year to train staff in the finer culinary arts of the East. Chefs at a live pasta station perform every lunch and dinner. The buffet spreads are adventurous and perfectly turned out.

A grill specialising in lobster, squid, prawn and steaks has a fine spot at the water's edge and serves just four tables: three candlelit on the beach and one on the beach bar decking.

For service, cuisine and a fun but always genteel holiday, Taj Coral Reef scores highly.

| 1 | 2 | 3 | 4 | 5 | 6 | 7 | **8** | 9 | 10 | | 1 | 2 | 3 | **4** | 5 | 6 | 7 | 8 | 9 | 10 |

LOWEST   RELATIVE PRICE   HIGHEST   MOST   ROOM DENSITY   LEAST

T 664 2200 F 664 2211
E roomrsvn@tajexotica.com.mv
www.tajhotels.com

South Male Atoll

 15 mins

 $7.70

 $5.50

 $7.70

 $132

 $66

Dolphin Base

 $90

5 x $425

PADI $750

Taj Exotica

Taj Exotica is undoubtably in the top bracket of Maldives resorts with a niche in the sensory pleasures of well-being and good living - specifically, a world class spa and cuisine.

There are, of course, other selling points which aren't quite unique. Anyone arriving on a long-haul flight (and especially the night arrivals) will appreciate the fact that the resort is just a 15-minute luxury speedboat ride from the airport. This proximity also enables the special submarine and seaplane excursions (for a complete view of the country) as well as easy access to Male for the historical tour.

Big Game Fishing can also be arranged but other excursions are more along the lines of private sunset or starlight cruises, for Exotica is essentially a slow, ultra-calm place where people glide around in their own romantic couple space. The simplicity of the island and its surroundings work to accentuate this.

The huge lagoon with its soft, white base shines out a shade of turquoise that is at once uplifting and calming. Set in the middle of this vast seascape is the thread of sand and vegetation that is Embudu Finolhu, the island's native name. At the southern tip is the spa; near it is the specialty restaurant and the swimming pool. Then come the land rooms, the bar, the reception and jetty and finally the main restaurant, all looking west to the sunset. On the other side is the library followed by the waterbungalows running the length of the east side.

56 of the 62 rooms in total are waterbungalows, split between 24 Lagoon Villas, 21 Deluxe Lagoon Villas, ten Deluxe Lagoon Villas with plunge pool and one Presidential Rehendhi Suite. They vary in size and detail but essentially share the same design and furniture. The style is rich, substantial and refined but never overstated. The oatmeal and light yellow tones of the fabrics and walls offset the formality of the teak furniture and decor. The first of the Lagoon Villas have the hum and edge view of the service area and a number of the Deluxe Lagoon Villas have the lights of Male on the horizon, but otherwise the views are unbounded.

The land rooms have the luxury of extra space, outdoor shade and an over-sized plunge pool with decking on three sides and the beach on the other. The path down the centre of the island runs behind the rooms though guests often prefer to stroll along the beach in front. The beach itself is broad, pure white and slopes imperceptibly into the lovely lagoon. Beach connoisseurs would note it is not the very softest Maldives can offer.

The truly sublime aspects of Taj Exotica are the haute cuisine and the spa. Individually they are in the top three or four in the country, together they make a compelling case to fly half the way around the world.

The Jiva Grande Spa is the premium spa product of the Taj Group. As such it eschews any pretence or window dressing. This is a spa with a thoroughgoing, Indian-based philosophy with integrated treatments, exercises and diets. It also looks great - under thatch by the sea, surrounding a floral courtyard. The exercises are yoga and meditation with the in-house teacher (a glass-walled gym is over-water just outside). The diets and the treatments are worked through with the ayurvedic doctor. The treatments may be strictly ayurvedic for specific conditions or focused on relaxation, cleansing and beauty. The signature offering is drawn from an Indian bathing ritual and involves anointing with therapeutic mud, essential oils and Experience Showers.

Although most people are on full board every meal is à la carte. For the ideals of presentation, integrity and freshness the single plate precisely prepared by the chef is the only way. For extra variety, some nights of the week there are extended set menus and also specials such as 'Wok around the world' and 'Feed me, Asian tasting'. Then, beyond this, there is a line at the bottom of the menu that says if you have a dietary preference the chefs will be happy to take care of it. This takes the options to infinity. If you would like a complicated lobster menu for dinner, just mention it at lunchtime.

The main restaurant covers the whole gamut of Asian cuisine. The specialty restaurant is very fine dining around Western and Mediterranean cuisine. If there is a house style it is beyond nouvelle cuisine, beyond fusion and molecular and back to rejuvenated mother's cooking! Or put another way, it is elevating and redefining traditional regional cuisines. And mother never presented a plate like this.

By the way, the bar is one of the best looking in the country and the library is the best in the country. For those pleasures of the body and the mind, Taj Exotica has its own perfect niche.

T 668 0583 F 668 0515
E admin@thudufushi.com.mv
www.planhotel.ch

1	2	3	4	**5**	6	7	8	9	10

LOWEST RELATIVE PRICE HIGHEST

1	2	3	**4**	5	6	7	8	9	10

MOST ROOM DENSITY LEAST

South Ari Atoll

25 mins

inc

inc

inc

$30

$15

The Crab

$83

6 x $457

PADI $625

Thudufushi

Thudufushi has a sister island, the nearby Athuruga, and almost everything said about that resort is relevant to this one too.

They are both similarly sized (just under 50 rooms) and shaped (roughly round, on the edge of their own lagoon). The level of maintenance on both is top notch and they offer probably the best standard of all-inclusive in the country.

Both resorts do all-inclusive holidays only and the differences between them are subtle matters of lifestyle and atmosphere. These, in turn, reflect the differences in clientele. In comparison to Athuruga, Thudufushi is more distinctly a club, more 'all-together' and with rather more emphasis on looks and style. This would be due to Italians making up eight out of ten guests for much of the year. It is friendly and great fun but perhaps a little less easygoing.

The front-office staff wear a very smart, quasi-colonial outfit. The barmen and waiters wear sarongs during the day and long, white Indian kurtas in the evening. The European staff and management wear the smart casual uniform of the club colours. The setting is refined and formal, as any upper class club might be, but the atmosphere is informal: there is constant banter between the staff and guests, plenty of chatter and laughter. During the day it's swimwear, wraps and bare feet, but in the evening guests return from their rooms dressed and made up for the pre-prandial get-together.

The evening meal starts later here than it does on Athuruga and the talking and drinking last longer into the night. In the same way, the daytime excursions leave later too, for this is essentially an Italian resort. Mealtimes are gregarious affairs and the food is splendid. From the open kitchen to the barbecuing fish on the beach, it is a nightly feast for the eyes and the taste buds. Afterwards, guests gather once more for the night's cabaret, put on by the European staff.

The restaurant, cabaret, beach bar and public areas front a fine beach on the west side of the island. This is the obvious place for everyone to gather and enjoy each other's company throughout the day. The rooms facing east into the open water have a reduced beach with some erosion issues (and only morning sunshine), whilst those on the north and south enjoy splendid bulges of exquisite sand.

As is the Italian preference, all the rooms are outside the canopy, with open views of the water and direct access to the beach. The downside to this is that there is a lack of privacy, with every room in clear view of its neighbours. You can't have everything.

Inside, the rooms are spacious, solid and well equipped, with a range of complementary toiletries, double basin and bidet, dressing gown, wooden clothes hangers, comfortable chairs and broad verandah. A safe, hairdryer and full (free) minibar are included but not a tea/coffee maker, tv or CD player. 40 rooms are joined in pairs and seven are single.

The reef is ideal for a combination of snorkeling and watersports. For half the island it is just around 40 to 60 metres away, accessible at high tide almost anywhere but also with two channels cut through. On the other side, the lagoon opens out to afford a shallow and calm area for canoeing, windsurfing and cat sailing. And this, indeed, is where the watersports and beach bar are found.

The dive centre is found here too, in the thick of things, open and friendly, with a capacity for greater use. Generally it's one boat twice a day, with occasional night dives and full-day trips. The ratio of divers to instructors averages an excellent four or five and the system couldn't be easier on the guest: each diver's equipment is taken to the boat and returned, rinsed and hung up by dive base staff. The centre has achieved ISO certification, so assuring the highest levels of safety and procedures.

The island has a very fine canopy of mature palms over a quiet interior of soft sand and dappled sunlight. The Serena Spa is tucked away here, ethnic and alluring. A sizeable and nicely designed shopping arcade, not far away, is also alluring and takes you back out to the exterior of the island, to the fun, the sun and the togetherness.

| 1 | 2 | **3** | 4 | 5 | 6 | 7 | 8 | 9 | 10 |
| LOWEST | | RELATIVE PRICE | | HIGHEST |

| **1** | 2 | 3 | 4 | 5 | 6 | 7 | 8 | 9 | 10 |
| MOST | | | ROOM DENSITY | | | LEAST |

T 664 5930 F 664 5939
E reserve@thulhaagiri.com.mv
www.thulhaagiri.com.mv

North Male Atoll

	25 mins
	60 mins
	$3.30
	$3.65
	$3.85
1/2	$35
	$22
	Sub Aqua
	$64
5 x	$348
PADI	$450

Thulhagiri

For a small, quiet resort close to Male that is reasonably priced, Thulhagiri is a good choice.

During the high season there is a huge bulge of fine beach on the northwest side, where the first numbered rooms are. It narrows somewhat during the low season as the sand moves around the roughly circular island to the eastern side. The last 15 rooms or so have a permanent low coral wall in front, with two small steps down to the water's edge.

Again typically for these islands the lagoon is ideal: gently sloping from the beach it is sandy bottomed, always deep enough for swimming and neither too near nor too far from the reef edge. There are coral patches towards the drop-off that will satisfy children and beginner snorkelers, though the housereef itself is variable, with parts that are bare of corals and other areas that are good.

The 55 beach rooms are sited fairly close together around three quarters of the circle, with the bar, restaurant and reception building, the watersports centre and the dive school taking up rest of the perimeter. 17 waterbungalows lie in an arc leading off from the reception and face south.

More or less half the beach rooms are in connected blocks of three and the rest are individual. Built in an irregular pattern with some in front and some behind there will be preferences, but there is always a view of the beach and sea and it is only a matter of a few steps. This irregularity and the lack of defined concrete pathways through the shady interior gives the place less of a resort and more of a village feel, which certainly adds to its charm.

Inside the thatched rooms it is spacious, clean and simple. Decorated in tones of green to light yellow with screwpine woven panels and thick bamboo furniture they are not high design but they are just fine for their setting. The bathroom is neatly tiled and has a good size shower with a powerful spray.

The interior of the waterbungalows is more compact, with space taken up by the large bamboo armchairs and four-poster bed. French windows run around three sides of the room giving loads of light (though they can, of course, be curtained off). A wide verandah runs around two sides providing fine views and good privacy. Facing either south or west guests are assured of plenty of private sunbathing.

It must be that guests do spend a lot of time lingering in and around their rooms because despite there being a lot of rooms for the island's size it doesn't feel full or busy at all. The usual excursions are there but are not too much in demand and the watersports centre is large and well stocked but still mostly quiet. The dive school is a five-star PADI instructor centre but it is not one of the busiest around.

The mix of Germans, Swiss, Dutch and varied others seem to enjoy Thulhagiri for its peace and quiet, a sort of village homely feel. Like the pet budgerigars that happily chirp and multiply, everyone seems to love it here.

Great food always helps, of course, and Thulhagiri has long had a reputation for top class buffets. The resort is co-owned by the biggest supplier of fresh food to the resorts so you just have to add in good chefs and you are assured of fine dining.

Attached to the restaurant is the main bar (there is also a well positioned sunset bar). Low comfy chairs on the sandy floor under a high thatched roof give the place an informal setting to suit the style of the resort. Every evening there is some soft entertainment and then it's off to bed early - except perhaps for the live band night.

| 1 | 2 | 3 | 4 | 5 | **6** | 7 | 8 | 9 | 10 |

LOWEST   RELATIVE PRICE   HIGHEST

| 1 | **2** | 3 | 4 | 5 | 6 | 7 | 8 | 9 | 10 |

MOST   ROOM DENSITY   LEAST

T 664 3977 F 664 3397
E rsvn@vadoo.com.mv
www.vadoo.net

South Male Atoll

 20 mins

 55 mins

 $3.85

 $4.20

 $3.55

 $38

 $26

 Vadoo

 $50

5 x $242

PADI $741

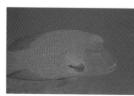

Vadoo

Vadoo is the epitome of small and quiet. There are just 24 rooms on the island and seven waterbungalows off it.

There are no watersports and no entertainment program. But it's not just small and quiet, it is also one of the last remaining resorts where nature is truly respected.

The resort was run for the first 18 years by Mr. Sakamoto, who spent 27 years in Maldives in all and recently returned to Japan. The prestige of the place is based upon its history (in a real sense 'his story'), and not upon the constant upgrading of buildings and facilities, the addition of more ticks in boxes. The success has been built by word-of-mouth reputation.

The canopy of trees and bushes has never been disturbed by major reconstruction. It looks good, the shade is cooling and, having never been sprayed, it is home to many birds. The leaves on the paths below are swept into the undergrowth (where most resorts now sweep the whole floor clean), which encourages other birds and wildlife. One gets the sense that wildlife feels safe here.

A resident naturalist carries out research as well as conducting tours for the guests. Since 2000 a regular 'Field Guide News' has been produced in Japanese and English, a fascinating source of information that guests can subscribe to for email delivery after they have left. And since 1992 the resort has been involved in valuable sea turtle research, which was recognised and formalised by the government three years later.

None of this is to say that the island is in some way precious or restrictively 'correct'. One can quite happily ignore all this and simply enjoy the delightfully natural and quiet setting. The emphasis is on feeling comfortable and at ease.

The seven Water Cottages include two suites, which have the addition of a second bedroom and lounge. The furnishing is a little old-fashioned but pleasant enough. Each of the wooden decks faces the sunset and has steps down to fine coral garden snorkeling. On this sunset side are also the eight Beach Cottages. On the east side are the 16 Sunrise Deluxe Rooms, which are relatively recent and so are bright, light and smart.

All the island rooms have good shading directly outside and then just a few steps through to a fine beach. The whole island enjoys a generous dose of deep, soft, fine sand. It also enjoys a nearby reef teeming with schools of fish, as well as baby sharks, blue fin jacks and plenty more. Sadly the coral regrowth has been disappointing here. The dive school, from where the snorkeling starts, maintains a constantly updated information board concerning current, visibility, temperature and what can be seen where. They also indicate the time and direction of the dolphins' morning and afternoon passages.

Diving has always been a key component of the resort. A high instructor to guest ratio ensures personal attention where required or desired and an unusually broad range of sites ensures diver satisfaction. There are six famous sites within ten minutes, including Vadoo Caves and Embudhu Express. The Victory Wreck is not far away to the north and the great Guraidhoo Channel is accessible to the south. The base leader, Iwasa, has been here for nine years lending stability and great local knowledge. However, the dive base itself looks like it could do with a bit of modernisation.

The restaurant has recently been altered to have an upper deck open to the stars (and a telescope to look at them). The buffets are not extensive (there are only 31 rooms) but the selection and taste is first class. An ayurvedic doctor adds his skills and knowledge to the natural setting and yoga is also now offered.

Enjoying it all is a majority of Japanese and a minority of Germans and others. It is really a place that everyone can enjoy - a piece of true Maldives.

1 2 3 4 **5** 6 7 8 9 10   1 2 3 4 **5** 6 7 8 9 10   T 668 0004 F 669 0007
LOWEST   RELATIVE PRICE   HIGHEST   MOST   ROOM DENSITY   LEAST   E reservations@vakaru.com
                                                                          www.vakaru.com

South Ari Atoll

 25 mins

120 mins

$3.50

$2.50

$4

$40

$15

ProDivers

$65

5 x $314

PADI $665

Vakarufalhi

Vakarufalhi has stayed just the same since it opened in 1994. While so much has moved on in Maldives, they simply decided not to change a winning formula, and watched as the others came back to them.

Thatch on all the roofs, sand on the floor throughout, good food, quality furnishings and high maintenance - that will do it every time. Of course if your natural environment is not good you might still struggle, but Vakarufalhi is blessed with mature vegetation, a truly great beach and a reef tight around the whole island.

It comes as no surprise that those who have discovered Vakarufalhi are frequent revisitors. Around two thirds of the guests are Swiss and Germans, one fifth British and the rest a mix of Italians and Scandinavians. A significant number are older than the average age in Maldives and stay for multiple weeks of winter sun and relaxation. A significant number are also heavily into diving. This profile makes perfect sense in a set-up designed for total relaxation and great diving.

It is rare good fortune to have a beach that goes all the way around the island, deep and fine without any pumping. Each of the rooms enjoys a lovely prospect of the beach and lagoon but is, at the same time, well shaded by mature palms and its own thatched roof overhanging the verandah. The verandahs themselves are extensions of the beach, only enclosed and swept (and occasionally traversed by grey herons).

With this beach you can't go far wrong with a room choice, though the first ten face northeast and the beach has a distinct slope. This is also where the all-surrounding sea wall is closest. The south and west sides, where the rest of the 50 rooms are located, enjoy a much greater distance to that sea wall. That is one thing that has changed over the years but is the price paid for a permanent, all-island, ideal beach.

Housereef snorkeling is accessed off the end of the two jetties (one each side of the island) and it's perfectly possible to swim all the way around. The reef has been strangely slow to recover its corals but the fish life is decent. Highlights are the batfish, reef sharks, turtles and schools of blue-striped snappers. Italians are lucky to have their own biologist to explain all the good things in the water and on land.

Set back in the middle of Dhigurah Channel, one of the most famous channels in the country, the divers here are spoilt for choice. There are more than 15 thila dives within a 20-minute radius. That's good for partners who don't dive and don't want to be alone all day - unless, that is, the partner has taken one of the frequent all-day trips!

Whale sharks are the big prize on the outside sites and, from January to March, there is a very productive Manta Point on the west of the atoll.

The ProDivers centre is run in a very friendly and personal manner, partly due to the number of repeaters and also part of the reason why there are so many repeaters. There are various other incentives to keep coming back, culminating in the gift of free diving for the whole of your tenth visit.

As is expected of an island of divers and relaxers, there isn't any emphasis on evening entertainments, all-together excursions and activities. The bar, with its floral cushions, low lighting and dark wood varnish, is like a small 'olde worlde' pub but in no sense is it the centre of life, even on those crazy crab racing nights. There are daily fishing trips and sunset dolphin cruises and then a mix of snorkeling trips and island excursions.

An unpretentious spa, made entirely of thatch and woven panels of screwpine leaves, has a lovely location right on the edge of the beach. Small, neat and fun, it offers a good range of massages and some beauty treatments and has the backing of a number of Duniye Spas already in the country.

Vakarufalhi is a now a great resort, comfortable with itself and what it offers. As long as you don't crave for a bit of music, dance and action you can't go wrong here.

T 666 0551 F 666 0630
E velidhu@dhivehinet.net.mv
www.johnkeellshotels.com

| 1 | 2 | **3** | 4 | 5 | 6 | 7 | 8 | 9 | 10 | | 1 | 2 | 3 | 4 | **5** | 6 | 7 | 8 | 9 | 10 |
| LOWEST | | RELATIVE PRICE | | | HIGHEST | | | | | | MOST | | | ROOM DENSITY | | | | | LEAST | |

North Ari Atoll

 25 mins

 90 mins

 330 mins

 $3.30

 $3.85

 $3.85

½ $30

 $28

 Eurodivers

 $67

5 x $302

PADI $523

Velidhu

This resort is one of Maldives' surprising success stories. It's not beautiful but it's very popular, aided by an admirably committed management and staff.

Despite a (low) wall in the lagoon around two thirds of the island and frequent groynes, the beaches outside the rooms are not good. There are requests for room changes to be by the good beach but the unfortunate thing is that most of the really good stretch of wide sand doesn't have any rooms on it but is fronted by the large and spread out reception and bar.

But as Hans, the dive base leader, told me, people are happy here. And that seemed to be true. One good reason would be Hans himself and the great diving to be had in the neighbourhood. Of a German dive magazine's top 100 sites in the world, three can be visited from here. So too can Maldives' only known hammerhead shark site (Rasdhoo).

Run by Eurodivers, there is an emphasis on detailed briefings and suitability. Each day's dives are posted on a board with an indication of whether they are for beginners, advanced or the experienced. With its reputation in the German market in particular, there are more than the average number of experienced divers. As well as the two morning and afternoon boats there are frequent special dives.

The main jetty is the only access point for snorkeling but the extent and quality of the snorkeling is very good.

Something over two thirds of the guests are from Germany, up to 20% from Italy and the remainder mostly from the U.K. Not much goes on in the daytime but the bar is full at night and most evenings there is entertainment such as a DJ, karaoke, magic show and local music. With nearly two-thirds on all-inclusive packages the evenings can be long ones, but it is never rowdy here. If the guests are not rich, there is an air of respectability.

A little indication of this is the fact that many couples prefer to dress up a bit for dinner. And the dinner doesn't let them down. It has greatly improved over the last few years to the point of being very good. Being inside the island, there are no views to sea and no chance for beach dinners, except as a specialty from the small waterfront Barbecue Grill.

The restaurant, bar and reception all have the same decorative elements of pillars and 'branches' lashed together or wrapped around with thick coir rope. They are far from homely yet not grand either - an odd cross between nautical neatness and desert island style.

The seemingly haphazard layout of the island is partly explained by four separate room building periods: first 30 Beach Bungalows, then another 30, then another 20 and then, more recently, 20 Waterbungalows.

All the Beach Bungalows are essentially the same but some are distinctly better placed than others. Experience will tell you which ones are close to or behind others and which ones are more or less on their own. All of them are good rooms built in a pleasingly different circular shape. Nothing fancy, they are reasonably large, comfortable and in good order.

The Waterbungalows are decorated to appear rather more rich and fancy. It is all a bit too green inside but they are unquestionably large, and the sizeable verandah on three sides has good privacy. Oddly there are no steps down to the water but one must walk to the sundeck at the end of the waterbungalow jetty for the ladder. Half the rooms face west and half east.

Velidhu is much better than its parts. There are design issues and the island isn't the prettiest but people do really enjoy their holidays here. An upfront, committed staff, good food, good snorkeling and great diving, plus that intangible of other similar, friendly people, all at a good price, combine to make this a big success story.

T 666 0519 F 666 0648
E reservations@veliganduisland.com
www.veliganduisland.com

1	2	3	4	5	**6**	7	8	9	10		**1**	2	**3**	4	5	6	7	8	9	10
LOWEST		RELATIVE PRICE				HIGHEST					MOST				ROOM DENSITY				LEAST	

Rashdoo Atoll

20 mins

$3.50

$2.50

$4

$35

$18

Ocean Pro

$66

5 x $330

PADI $619

Veligandu

As resorts upgrade and expand they sometimes lose the original Maldives feel. Not Veligandu. It still has white sand on the floors, thatched roofs above and a calm, friendly atmosphere.

It also boasts a sandbank that is a serious tanner's dream. Indeed, it gives the resort its name - 'Veligandu' means sandbank in dhivehi. A long tongue of the softest sand extends out from the main body of the island. Open to the sun all day but dotted with thatched umbrellas, it is never more than a few steps to the sparkling lagoon on either side.

Every land room has some degree of beach, with the Superior Bungalows on the west side (130-149) enjoying the largest, and ever growing, bulge. These would be just preferable to the Superiors facing the rising sun, on the other side of this narrow north/south directed island.

The eight Deluxe Bungalows used to be water-bungalows, which just shows how much the beach has been growing. They are built in pairs, one of which (128/9) is not in a great position behind bushes and a little shore wall. The other three pairs are in a quiet corner on the east side away from the other rooms, though they do look out to the only built sea walls (mostly covered at high tide).

The Deluxe Rooms are larger and have a private wooden deck, plus a tea/coffee and espresso maker. Otherwise, both room types are equally light, clean and well appointed, with full minibar, CD player and a third bed as standard.

There are ten original Water Villas and 12 new Deluxe Water Villas. The Deluxe are longer and wider, have a partly open bathroom and a larger wooden deck with greater privacy than the Water Villas, but, on the other hand, they are less 'of a piece'. They are darker, with a dark varnished floor (conflicting with the light pine walls) and daylight coming from only one side. Only one narrow door is usually open to the deck (though the whole thing can be opened) in comparison to the double doors of the regular Water Villas. Both bathrooms are good, with double basins and a great massage shower - where, here again, the Deluxe Rooms are slightly less good with one not two lumber sprays because of their glass wall design.

The Serena Spa is another new addition that fits right in with the relaxed and relaxing Veligandu concept. Built in the Indian style, there's Indian classical music and patchouli or sandalwood incense in the air. The massage strokes are based on the Indian tradition, with ayurveda and aromatherapy options as well as a selection of body scrubs, wraps and polishes. An unsurprisingly popular therapy is one called The Sunlovers' Package, which is developed around a coconut oil rehydration. The Adam and Eve Serenity is another favourite in the dual therapy room.

The food has always been a strength of the resort; it still is and now the setting is even more pleasant. The handsome thatched roof curves over the restaurant and bar, white sand covers the floor and the solid tables are complimented by good-looking modern chairs. Breakfasts are up there with the best, lunches are buffets and dinners are either a changing menu of theme buffets or à la carte. There is always the option of eating outside on the wide deck that sweeps around the restaurant and bar.

The resort is a fine diving location. With just one other resort, Kuramathi, in this small atoll and many good spots, the boat trips are mostly within 25 minutes and you're mostly alone. A good manta point is just to the north (usually December to May), but the highlight is certainly the hammerhead shark point. It's a 6am start but the dive base leader Ole almost shudders as he says he never fails to get excited, it's something about the way they move. A two-tank dive is a regular option down to north Ari Atoll, to Maya Thila, one of the top spots in the country. With four other types of sharks not infrequently noted on these trips it's unsurprising a shark specialty course is offered back at base.

Snorkeling is not possible from the rooms but is pretty good from the main jetty and the jetty at the end of sand spit. It is very good on the ocean side but this is only accessible from the dive boat or resort snorkel excursion. One excursion is of particular note. Hoodoo is an inhabited island on its own tiny atoll some kilometres north of Veligandu. For this reason it is rarely visited but it's a special place: traditional, friendly, a rare agricultural island and the site of equally rare ancient Buddhist remains.

All in all what you have here is a smart yet informal island under good management; a place that looks good, feels good and does you good.

1	2	**3**	4	5	6	7	8	9	10
LOWEST		RELATIVE PRICE			HIGHEST				

1	2	**3**	4	5	6	7	8	9	10
MOST		ROOM DENSITY					LEAST		

T 668 0637 F 668 0639
E vilamendhu@aaa.com.mv
www.aaa-resortsmaldives.com

South Ari Atoll

25 mins

$3.50

$3.30

$4.50

$30

$15

Werner Lau

$73

6 x $418

PADI $686

Vilamendhoo

Vilamendhoo has a few key things going for it. It has unmatched access to snorkeling and housereef diving, all the rooms are near the water's edge, the food is good and the overall price is very reasonable.

The east - west lay of the island, with channels to the north and south, means you get bulges of sand on the tips but it is difficult to keep beach along the sides. And as it is no longer acceptable for the bulges of sand to shift from one season to the other, there are now a considerable number of land walls and lagoon walls, variously visible and disjointed. The upside is there has been no pumping of sand from the lagoon (there isn't anywhere to pump it from) and so the beaches are of a lovely quality.

The ten Deluxe Rooms are located at the two tips, so enjoying the best of the beaches. Around the rest of the island run the 131 Superior Rooms. Location is the only real difference between the two categories (tea/coffee, hairdryer, a bathtub but no stand-alone shower). There are also 13 Standard Rooms in the interior.

The public buildings are tight and angular. They are somewhat dark without open sides and only the sunset bar has sand on the floor - all the other places being tiled. It's a bit of a giveaway that guests are mostly seen on deck-chairs outside the bars and tv lounge.

Germans make up something over half the guests here, with British around a third and the remainder being mostly French and Italians. It is noticeable that there is a full spread of ages, from retirees to children (of whom there are more in the high season). Around three quarters of the guests are on all-inclusive but that has not meant a reduction in the quality of the cuisine. On the contrary, the food on Vilamendhoo has improved dramatically and is now excellent for this level of resort. This always goes a long way to keeping people happy.

For Maldives, another key to keeping guests happy is good diving and accessible snorkeling and for that Vilamendhoo scores very highly. This resort has probably the shortest distance between the rooms and the reef of any in the country. And with ten cut-throughs to the drop-off it is wonderfully accessible. (One should also be mindful that the cut-throughs are a compromise with the reef and the beach).

Apart from day and night housereef diving, the quality of sites in this area is still superb. This is the most renowned area for diving in Ari Atoll. Although the dive school is well set up for new courses, the sites in general are for advanced divers, with many Werner Lau devotees coming back year after year. In the high season the visibility is excellent and the pelagic fish-life top class around the channel thilas. The current, though, is sometimes strong to very strong. In the off-season the current is weaker and visibility less good but then the divers head out to the south and west of the atoll to see the mantas and whale sharks.

The resort recently went through a period when maintenance was not prioritised. This was due to an ownership dispute which is now cleared up. Vilamendhoo may change significantly in the future but it's core selling points will remain: the snorkeling and the diving are excellent.

| 1 | 2 | 3 | 4 | 5 | 6 | 7 | 8 | 9 | 10 |
LOWEST   RELATIVE PRICE   HIGHEST

| 1 | 2 | 3 | 4 | 5 | 6 | 7 | 8 | 9 | 10 |
MOST   ROOM DENSITY   LEAST

T 676 0011 F 676 0022
E info@vilureef.com.mv
www.vilureef.com

Dhaalu Atoll

 35 mins

 inc

 inc

 $4.40

 $40

 $20

 Sun International

 $65

6 x $372

PADI $695

Vilu Reef

Vilu Reef is wonderfully endowed by nature. A good reef is close by on one side for snorkeling; a sandy lagoon on the other side is perfect for watersports.

A wide, white beach goes all the way around. Furthermore, unusually good soil supports dense vegetation, with many flowers and tall coconut palms.

That there are just too many rooms for the island's size is the one thing that detracts from this ideal picture. More than a few of the 62 Beach Villas have hindered views to the beach. Inside the island are 20 Garden Villas and outside lie 41 waterbungalows.

The rooms themselves are attractive and well put together. The Beach Villas are a good size, thatched, shell-shaped, with a walk-in wardrobe and extra bed/sofa. Outside is an extended wooden deck, with cushioned loungers and thatched umbrella, that creates a pleasant and private space.

Of the waterbungalows 35 are Jacuzzi Water Villas, five are Honeymoon Water Villas and one is a Presidential Water Suite. The jacuzzi bath is on the large outside deck, which also has a useful shaded area. Privacy is total, which is excellent, though it does mean there is somewhat less light inside the rooms. The Honeymoon Water Villas, on the other hand, have a separate living room with glass walls on three sides, though privacy is still maintained.

At the top of the island, at the base of the water-bungalow jetty, is a smart new facility combining swimming pool, bar and à la carte sunset restaurant, which also hosts the special dinners such as 'The Romantic Menu' and the 'Lobster Dinner'. All options, including the sports and excursions, are well advertised with laminated pictures on a board outside the reception.

The beach is wide, fine and lovely where it exists, which is most of the way around. The southern tip is particularly good and, facing the sun during the day, these are the rooms to go for. Other rooms facing west to the setting sun also have a fine beach, but the shoreline narrows around the northern tip so a short but highish lagoon wall has been built here.

The bar and lounge has a fine, swirling thatched roof, cowrie shell decoration and muted turquoise shell textiles over low-slung wicker chairs on a white sandy floor. The mix of the grand and the easygoing is just right. The wooden deck outside faces west for the perfect sundowner. The restaurant is segmented so one isn't so aware of the number of people all together and the food is good.

A further factor that reduces the sense of crowding is the gardening. A particular interest of the former general manager, the growth of trees, bushes and flowers is as good here as any other resort and better than most. The path around the interior is green, shady and calming. Tucked in the middle of this greenery is the excellent spa. Unsurprisingly it is very popular. The therapists, many of the treatments and the decorative touches are all from India. It's a quiet, open, airy place of natural materials, with lovely smells and relaxing sounds.

Snorkeling is another strong point of the resort, with plenty of coral inside the lagoon and good access through to the always reachable reef drop-off. However, as it is at the edge of a fast-flowing channel care must be taken to check the prevailing conditions. With just one other resort in this atoll and one in the atoll above (as of 2007), the dive sites are still pristine and 'fully stocked'. Like many centres now, nitrox dives and courses are offered.

German speakers and British are the majority guests around the year, though Italians and Japanese are numerous in the high season months. Almost everyone is all-inclusive, which is the ordinary package - except Italians get a little less and no one gets a free sunset fishing.

The resort is particularly good for children, with lots of shade, baby-sitting, the extra bed, a little park and, above all, a good attitude throughout. The resort also offers wedding vow renewal packages and honeymoon extras so Vilu Reef is really a place for everyone.

T 668 0513 F 668 0512
E resort@maldiveswhitesands.com
www.maldiveswhitesands.com

1	2	3	4	5	**6**	7	8	9	10
LOWEST		RELATIVE PRICE		HIGHEST					

1	2	3	4	**5**	6	7	8	9	10
MOST			ROOM DENSITY				LEAST		

South Ari Atoll

25 mins

180 mins

$5.50

$4.85

$6.05

½ $31

$28

Eurodivers

$55

5 x $261

PADI $554

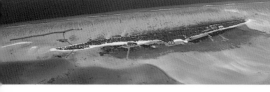

White Sands

In the short history of Maldives tourism this island has a long tradition. It was the epitome of the simple, easygoing, natural life - "no news, no shoes" was first used here.

Every floor was sand, every wall was of coral and every roof was thatched. It is no longer quite like that, as new owners come and renovations are made, yet I sense the special feeling is still here. An uncommon mix of ages (honeymooners, young couples, families, some elderly) and nationalities get along very happily - sometimes active, sometimes chilling and sometimes having a bit of fun.

Over time a convenient pattern has developed on this long island. One end is where most of the fun and games happen and as you progress up the island it becomes more reserved and smarter right up to the private world of the waterbungalows off the other end of the island.

A typical night in the Nagili Bar might have a sarong wearing competition followed by a little dance show by the all-female troupe of guest relations officers and activities managers. On another night the crowd is drawn out to the beach for a disco under the stars. A nicely done newssheet keeps everyone informed about what's happening the next day.

At this end of the island are the standard rooms, called Island Guest Rooms (28) and Junior Suites or family rooms (14). Standard today, of course, means well-finished rooms with all the mod cons, and these are decent rooms though a little on the small side and close to the neighbours.

Further along the sandy path as the island narrows you come to the 50 Beach Cottages, which are 'A' frame houses split into two rooms and a distinct step up in terms of space, privacy and interior design. The bathroom is notably good, with deep tub, power shower and slate tiles.

Long islands often have narrow beaches along their sides and this one is no exception but these rooms, particularly the last ones (the 240s & 250s), have plenty to keep their occupants happy. The beach then blossoms out at the tip of the island where you find the beach bar, the watersports centre and an ample number of sunloungers and umbrellas.

The watersports centre is one of best stocked and most actively run in the country.

Before leaving the island along the waterbungalow jetty, I should talk about a surprising star of the resort, the Coconut Spa. This is the lead spa of the three that the company runs in Maldives (the others being on Reethi Beach and Angaga). It boasts a fine location on the beach and it is better looking than the other two but those things are not its big draw. It is the welcome and the consideration by the manager and the skill of the Balinese therapists that have people raving about it.

Stephanie, the manager (and owner's daughter), calls it a family atmosphere where it's OK to laugh and joke and where people are always welcome to drop in and have a cup of flavoured tea even if they are not taking a treatment. The only downside is you are close to a stranger in a smallish room with a screen if you haven't come as a couple.

Couples' massages are very popular with the many honeymooners who come here to stay in the delightful waterbungalows. For utter privacy there are two set adrift in the lagoon and only reachable by boat. The other 50 are strung along a zigzag walkway and include three double-size suites.

With their outward sloping walls they are shaped like some officers room in a fine old galleon. The interior design is a most tasteful mix of woods and cottons. Clearly and rightfully the premium rooms on the resort. The sundecks are hidden from their neighbours but the lagoon in front is very shallow at low tide. And, as elsewhere on the island, there is no decent snorkeling to talk of.

Diving remains very popular here for understandable reasons. This is the southeast section of Ari Atoll that is world famous for its great dive sites. Whale sharks are regulars at the right time of year. Although the dive centre is small it is surprisingly comprehensive with what it offers, though not too surprising perhaps for a five-star instructor development centre.

White Sands carries on the rustic, easygoing tradition of Ari Beach (its predecessor) and brings the facilities bang up-to-date. And it still has that special feeling.

With over 87 dream islands to choose from let us find you the Maldivian Paradise you deserve

We have more than 17 years experience, reach the place you've always desired at the right price

SUN TRAVELS & TOURS PVT. LTD.

Crown Tours
Your idea of the lifetime travel experience!

Personalized Holiday Planning

Whether on one resort or over several resorts; or combine your resort stay with a cruise. Our customer-tailored holidays offer you the choice of more than one Maldivian experience.

Fasmeeru Building 5th Flr, Boduthakurufaanu Magu P.O. Box 2034, Male, Republic of Maldives
Tel: +960 332 9889, Fax: +960 331 2832, Email: sales@crowntoursmaldives.com
www.crowntoursmaldives.com

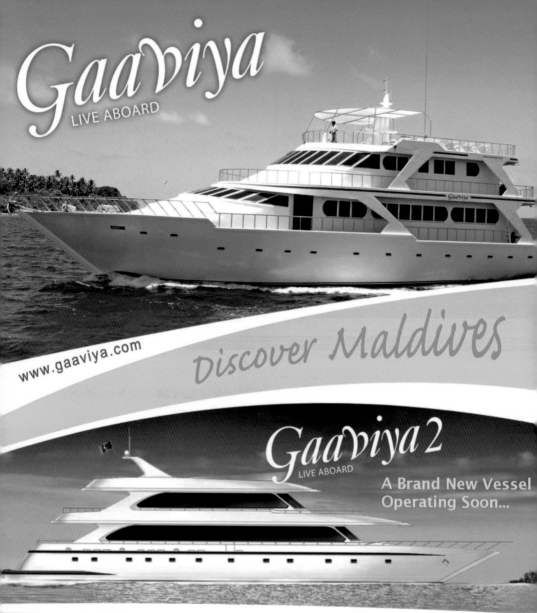

Pulished by SevenHolidays
adrian@sevenholidays.com

First edition : 1998
Second edition : 2002
Third edition(guidebook format) : 2007

ISBN : 978-0-9556043-0-0

Written and photographed by Adrian Neville
Designed by Boyd & Co
Printed by Samhwa, Seoul, Korea